Timeless Pickling and Fermenting

Culinary Skills for the Survivalist

Mia Patel

Table of Contents

INTRODUCTION

In an era characterized by quick technological advancements and an ever-accelerating pace of life, a timeless culinary art stands as a beacon of tradition, sustainability, and self-sufficiency: pickling and fermenting. Rooted in ancient practices dating back thousands of years, these methods of food preservation have not only sustained civilizations through lean times but continue to offer invaluable skills for modern survivalists seeking to thrive in uncertain times. Welcome to "Timeless Pickling and Fermenting: Culinary Skills for the Survivalist."

This book is a comprehensive guide to the art and science of pickling and fermenting, explicitly tailored to the needs and interests of those prioritizing self-reliance and sustainability. Within these pages, you will embark on a voyage through the rich history, fundamental principles, and practical techniques that underpin these age-old culinary traditions.

Pickling and fermenting are not merely culinary endeavors; they are deeply ingrained in the fabric of human culture and survival. From the ancient civilizations of Mesopotamia and China to the homesteads of pioneer settlers, pickled and fermented foods have played a vital part in nourishing communities and preserving harvests for leaner times. Today, as we confront global challenges such as climate change, food insecurity, and economic uncertainty, the wisdom of these time-honored practices is more relevant than ever.

In the following chapters, we will delve into the intricacies of pickling and fermentation, exploring the diverse array of foods that can be preserved through these methods, from crisp cucumbers to tangy sauerkraut, and from zesty kimchi to robust sourdough bread. Along the way, we will uncover the health benefits, nutritional value, and environmental advantages of incorporating pickled and fermented foods into our diets.

Whether you are a seasoned homesteader, a curious novice, or simply someone seeking to reduce food waste and embrace a more sustainable lifestyle, "Timeless Pickling and Fermenting" offers a wealth of knowledge, inspiration, and practical advice to help you harness the power of these ancient culinary arts in your own kitchen. Join us as we rediscover the joys of preserving the harvest, nurturing our bodies, and connecting with the timeless rhythms of nature through the transformative magic of pickling and fermenting.

CHAPTER I

Understanding Pickling and Fermenting

Definition of pickling and fermenting

Pickling and fermenting are two ancient methods of food preservation that have played a critical role in human culinary practices across cultures and time periods. These methods not only extend the shelf life of perishable foods but also enhance their flavors, nutritional values, and digestibility. Despite their similarities, pickling and fermenting are distinct processes with unique mechanisms and outcomes. This section delves into the definitions, methods, and cultural significances of pickling and fermenting, shedding light on how these age-old techniques continue to be integral to our dietary practices.

Pickling is known as a method of preserving food by means of immersing it in an acidic solution, typically vinegar, or fermenting it in a salt brine, eventually producing the necessary acidic conditions. The primary goal of pickling is to inhibit the growth of bacteria, yeasts, and molds that cause food spoilage, thereby extending the food's shelf life. The acidic environment created during the pickling process prevents the proliferation of these microorganisms, while the spices and seasonings enhance the flavors of the food often added to the pickling mixture. Pickling can be applied to various foods, including vegetables, fruits, meats, and even eggs. The practice of pickling dates back thousands of years, with evidence of pickled foods found in ancient Mesopotamia.

Over the centuries, it has become a staple in many culinary traditions worldwide, each culture developing its unique pickling recipes and methods that reflect local tastes and available ingredients.

Fermenting, on the other hand, is a preservation technique that relies on the action of specific types of bacteria, yeasts, or fungi to convert organic substances in food into alcohol, acids, or gases. This process preserves the food and creates distinctive flavors, textures, and health benefits. Fermentation typically occurs under anaerobic conditions, where the lack of oxygen encourages the growth of beneficial microorganisms that are naturally present on the food or are introduced through a starter culture. These microorganisms metabolize sugars and other carbohydrates in the food, producing lactic acid, alcohol, and carbon dioxide, which act as natural preservatives. Fermented foods are renowned for their probiotic properties, offering various health benefits, which includes improved digestion and enhanced immune function. Fermentation has been utilized across various cultures for millennia, giving rise to beloved foods such as yogurt, sauerkraut, kimchi, sourdough bread, and kombucha, among others.

While pickling and fermenting serve the purpose of food preservation, the processes and outcomes of each method are distinct. Pickling generally involves adding an acidic solution to food, quickly creating an environment hostile to spoilage-causing microorganisms. This method can preserve the food for an extended period without necessarily altering its nutritional content significantly. Fermenting, however, involves a more complex biological process where microorganisms directly transform the food's chemical composition. This transformation often results in the creation of new nutrients, such as B vitamins, and the enhancement of the food's digestibility and nutritional absorption.

Culturally, pickling and fermenting have deep roots in various societies, embodying the ingenuity of human adaptation to preserve food before the advent of modern refrigeration. These methods reflect the geographical, environmental, and cultural contexts of different regions, showcasing the diversity of human cuisine. For example, the spicy and pungent flavors of Korean kimchi reflect the use of local ingredients and the cultural importance of fermentation in Korean culinary traditions. Similarly, the practice of pickling cucumbers in Eastern Europe has resulted in a wide array of pickled cucumber varieties, each with its unique taste and texture, symbolizing the region's historical and cultural identity.

In contemporary times, there has been a resurgence of interest in pickling and fermenting, driven by a growing awareness of their health benefits, the desire for sustainable food preservation methods, and an interest in artisanal and traditional foods. This revival has encouraged both home cooks and professional chefs to experiment with these techniques, leading to innovative recipes and the re-discovery of traditional ones. Moreover, the community aspect of pickling and fermenting, where knowledge and cultures are shared, has contributed to their sustained popularity and relevance in today's culinary landscape.

In conclusion, pickling and fermenting are two fundamental food preservation methods that have shaped human dietary practices for millennia. While both aim to extend the shelf life of food, they do so through distinct processes that offer unique flavors, textures, and health benefits. Beyond their practical utility, pickling and fermenting are deeply embedded in cultural traditions worldwide, reflecting the diversity and creativity of human cuisine. As we continue to explore and embrace these ancient techniques, we not only connect with our past but also contribute to a more sustainable and health-conscious future.

Historical significance of pickling and fermenting

The historical significance of pickling and fermenting stretches far beyond their roles as mere food preservation techniques. These processes have been pivotal in the development of human civilization, enabling societies to thrive in harsh climates, support exploratory voyages, and contribute to the cultural and gastronomic diversity that characterizes global cuisines today. This section explores the deep historical roots of pickling and fermenting, their impact on human history, and how they have shaped culinary traditions worldwide.

The origins of pickling and fermenting can be traced back thousands of years, with proof suggesting that these methods were developed independently by various ancient civilizations. The practice of pickling, for example, is thought to have originated in ancient Mesopotamia around 2400 B.C., where cucumbers from India were preserved using brine. Similarly, fermenting has ancient roots, with records indicating that fermented beverages were consumed in ancient Egypt, Babylon, Mexico, and Sudan. These methods were not merely about preserving food; they were crucial innovations that allowed our ancestors to store surplus produce for times of scarcity, thereby enabling the establishment of settled communities and the development of agriculture.

The significance of pickling and fermenting in ancient times extended beyond sustenance. In many cultures, these preserved foods acquired symbolic meanings and became integral to religious rituals, festivals, and social customs. For instance, in ancient Greece, pickled vegetables were a staple in the diet and were associated with strength and stamina, leading athletes to consume them regularly. In Asia, fermented soy products like miso and soy sauce played vital roles in culinary traditions, their production techniques refined over centuries.

The historical impact of pickling and fermenting is also evident in their role in long-distance seafaring and exploration. Preserving food for extended periods was essential for the success of lengthy voyages. Pickled and fermented foods, rich in vitamins and resistant to spoilage, helped prevent scurvy among sailors and explorers, facilitating the age of exploration that expanded the geographical and cultural horizons of the ancient and medieval worlds. The global trade routes established during these times were not just conduits for spices and precious metals but also for the exchange of pickling and fermenting techniques, contributing to the cross-cultural culinary influences we see today.

Furthermore, the historical significance of these preservation methods is highlighted by their impact on societies' socio-economic development. In medieval

Europe, for example, the ability to store food through the winter months led to more stable communities, reduced the risks of famine, and supported population growth. In East Asia, the tradition of fermenting vegetables and fish contributed to dietary diversity and nutritional sufficiency, even during crop failure or economic hardship.

The Industrial Revolution and the advent of modern food preservation technologies in the 19th and 20th centuries did not diminish the importance of pickling and fermenting. Instead, these methods experienced a renaissance as part of a broader movement towards natural, organic, and sustainable food production. Today, the historical techniques of pickling and fermenting are celebrated for their health benefits, including probiotics that improve gut health and for their contributions to the richness of global culinary traditions.

In contemporary times, the revival of interest in pickling and fermenting is a testament to their enduring relevance. Artisanal producers and home cooks are exploring ancient recipes and techniques, adapting them to modern tastes and contributing to a global resurgence of fermented and pickled foods. This renewed interest is not merely a culinary trend but a recognition of these practices' deep historical roots and cultural significance.

The historical significance of pickling and fermenting is manifold, reflecting their roles in human survival, cultural development, and socio-economic stability. These ancient techniques, developed out of necessity, have evolved into cherished culinary traditions that enrich our diets and connect us to our past. As we continue to explore and innovate within the realms of pickling and fermenting, we pay homage to the ingenuity of our ancestors and the profound impact these practices have had on the course of human history. In doing so, we ensure that the legacy of pickling and fermenting remains vibrant, contributing to the diversity and sustainability of global food cultures for generations to come.

Importance of these skills for survivalists

The mastery of pickling and fermenting holds paramount importance for survivalists, individuals dedicated to preparing for and thriving in situations of uncertainty or survival scenarios. These ancient food preservation techniques, deeply rooted in human history, offer modern survivalists a means to extend the shelf life of perishable foods, enhance their nutritional value, and ensure a sustainable food source in environments where conventional preservation methods may not be feasible. This section delves into the significance of pickling and fermenting for survivalists, highlighting their food security, health, and self-sufficiency benefits.

In the context of survivalism, food preservation is a critical skill. The ability to store food for lengthy periods without reliance on electricity or modern refrigeration can be the difference between sustenance and starvation in crises. Pickling and fermenting stand out as viable solutions, enabling the safe preservation of various foods through natural processes. By immersing foods in vinegar or saltwater brine, pickling creates an acidic environment that inhibits the growth of spoilage-causing microorganisms. This method is not only effective for vegetables and fruits but also for meats and fish, providing a diverse range of nutrients essential for survival.

Fermenting, on the other hand, relies on the action of beneficial bacteria, yeasts, or fungi to convert sugars as well as starches in food into alcohol, acids, or gases. This process preserves the food and enhances its digestibility and nutritional profile, adding vital vitamins, minerals, and probiotics. For survivalists, fermented foods can be a crucial source of nutrition, improving gut health and boosting immunity, which is particularly important in stress-filled survival scenarios where the body's susceptibility to illness increases.

Moreover, the importance of pickling and fermenting for survivalists extends beyond mere nutrition and food preservation. These practices embody the self-sufficiency principle, a survivalist philosophy's core tenet. By mastering these techniques, survivalists can reduce their dependency on commercial food sources, which may be inaccessible or depleted in emergencies. Pickling and fermenting allow for the efficient use of local and foraged foods, enabling survivalists to adapt to their environment and make the most of available resources. This adaptability is crucial for thriving in diverse and potentially hostile environments, from wilderness areas to post-disaster urban landscapes.

The sustainability aspect of pickling and fermenting is another factor that underscores their importance for survivalists. These methods require minimal energy and resources compared to modern food preservation technologies, aligning with the survivalist ethos of minimizing waste and living in harmony with the environment. By utilizing renewable resources like salt, water, and natural fermenting agents, survivalists can ensure a continuous food supply with a low ecological footprint, an essential consideration for long-term survival planning.

In addition to practical benefits, pickling and fermenting have psychological and cultural significance for survivalists. Preserving food connects individuals to traditional knowledge and skills passed down through generations, fostering a sense of continuity and resilience. In times of uncertainty, the ability to produce and enjoy familiar, flavorful foods can offer comfort and improve morale among survivalists and their communities. This emotional and psychological support is invaluable in survival situations, where mental well-being is as crucial as physical health.

The skills of pickling and fermenting also promote community building and knowledge sharing among survivalists. Individuals can exchange techniques, recipes, and experiences by engaging in these practices, strengthening social bonds and creating a support network. This communal aspect can be instrumental in survival scenarios, where collaboration and shared resources significantly enhance the chances of success.

In conclusion, the importance of pickling and fermenting for survivalists cannot be overstated. These time-honored techniques provide a reliable means of food preservation, nutritional enhancement, and self-sufficiency, all of which are vital in survival contexts. By embracing these practices, survivalists equip themselves with the skills necessary to sustain life in adverse conditions, embodying the resilience and adaptability that define human survival across ages. As we move forward in an era marked by environmental challenges and societal uncertainties, the revival and mastery of pickling and fermenting stand as a testament to the enduring human spirit, offering a path toward sustainability, health, and resilience in the face of adversity.

CHAPTER II

Understanding Pickling

What is pickling?

Pickling, a method steeped in history and tradition, is a testament to human ingenuity in food preservation. It extends the shelf life of foods and enhances their flavors, contributing to the culinary diversity we enjoy today. This section explores the intricacies of pickling, its historical roots, methods, and the cultural significance that has cemented its place in cuisines worldwide.

Fundamentally, pickling is the process of preserving food through immersion in vinegar or anaerobic fermentation in brine. The underlying principle of pickling is to create an inhospitable environment for the microorganisms responsible for food spoilage. This is achieved through the acidification of the food's environment, which effectively halts the growth of spoilage-causing bacteria. The primary agents of this transformation are vinegar, a potent acid, and salt, which, in higher concentrations, serves as a preservative by drawing moisture out of the food and the microorganisms that could cause decay.

The origins of pickling trace back thousands of years, making it one of the oldest food preservation methods known to humanity. Historical records and archaeological evidence suggest that ancient civilizations, from Mesopotamia to China, practiced pickling to preserve surplus crops and ensure a stable food supply throughout the year. These early pickling practices were not only a necessity for survival but also paved the way for the development of diverse culinary traditions, as different cultures infused their pickled goods with various herbs, spices, and flavors unique to their regions.

The method of pickling varies widely across cultures, but all share the common goal of preservation through acidification. In one method, vegetables or fruits are submerged in vinegar, often flavored with a blend of spices, sugar, and salt, creating what is commonly called a "pickle." In another, the process of lacto-fermentation is employed, where salt is added to the produce to draw out water, creating a brine that facilitates the growth of beneficial bacteria, primarily Lactobacillus. These bacteria convert sugars in the food into lactic acid, naturally preserving the produce and imbuing it with a distinct sour flavor. This method is responsible for creating many of the world's fermented delicacies, such as sauerkraut, kimchi, and various pickled vegetables.

The benefits of pickling extend beyond preservation. The process can significantly enhance the nutritional profile of the preserved food. Fermented pickles, in particular, are a rich source of probiotics, beneficial bacteria that are crucial in gut health and digestion. Additionally, the spices and herbs often added during the pickling process can contribute additional nutrients and antioxidants, further enriching the food's health benefits.

Culturally, pickling has played a significant role in defining the culinary identities of various communities and regions. From Korea's spicy and tangy kimchi to the dill-infused pickles of Eastern Europe, pickled foods have become emblematic of national and regional cuisines, celebrated for their unique flavors and health benefits. Pickling traditions are often passed down through generations, preserving food, cultural heritage, and familial bonds.

In recent years, there has been a resurgence of interest in traditional pickling methods, driven by a growing appreciation for artisanal foods and the health benefits of fermented foods. Home cooks and professional chefs alike are experimenting with pickling, rediscovering ancient techniques, and incorporating pickled foods into modern dishes. This revival of interest speaks to the versatility and enduring appeal of pickling, highlighting its importance as a preservation method and a source of culinary innovation and creativity.

In conclusion, pickling is a multifaceted culinary art that marries the science of preservation with the rich tapestry of human culture and history. Its processes, whether through vinegar immersion or lacto-fermentation, offer a means to extend the life of perishable foods while enhancing their flavors and nutritional value. The practice of pickling reflects the ingenuity of our ancestors and continues to influence our dietary habits and culinary practices today. As we continue to explore and celebrate the diversity of pickled foods, we pay homage to our cultural heritage and contribute to our diets' sustainability and healthfulness. Pickling, in its essence, is a bridge between past and present, a tradition that nourishes both body and soul, making it an indispensable part of our culinary legacy.

Benefits of pickling

The art of pickling, an ancient food preservation technique, has transcended its initial purpose of extending the shelf life of perishable items, emerging as a practice rich in health, culinary, and environmental benefits. This multifaceted preservation method, characterized by the process of immersing foods in an acidic solution or through fermentation, has been recognized for its positive impact on nutritional value, taste enhancement, food waste reduction, and sustainability. This section delves into the myriad benefits of pickling, showcasing why it remains a cherished culinary tradition and a practical method for modern living.

One of the most lauded benefits of pickling is its contribution to enhancing the nutritional profile of foods. Fermented pickles, in particular, are a powerhouse of probiotics and beneficial bacteria such as Lactobacillus, which are known for their role in enhancing gut health. These probiotics emerge during fermentation, aiding digestion and enhancing the gut microbiota, which is crucial for maintaining overall health. The fermentation process also makes the nutrients in foods more bioavailable, meaning the body can absorb these nutrients more efficiently. For example, fermented vegetables can provide higher levels of vitamins B and C than their unfermented counterparts. Additionally, the brine or vinegar used in pickling can be a source of antioxidants as well as minerals, contributing further to the nutritional benefits of pickled foods.

Beyond health, pickling significantly enhances the culinary landscape by introducing an array of flavors and textures that can transform ordinary dishes into gourmet experiences. The acidic or salty environment of pickling creates a unique flavor profile, ranging from tangy and sour to sweet and spicy, depending on the spices and herbs used in the pickling process. This diversity allows chefs and home cooks alike to experiment with flavors, elevating the taste of meals and providing a creative outlet for culinary expression. Furthermore, the crunchy texture of pickled vegetables adds a pleasing contrast to dishes, making pickling a favorite technique among those looking to explore different sensory experiences in food.

From an environmental standpoint, pickling is a practical answer to the problem of food waste that exists worldwide. By preserving seasonal produce, individuals can reduce the amount of food discarded due to spoilage, thereby contributing to more sustainable consumption practices. This aspect of pickling is particularly relevant in today's context, where the environmental impact of waste is a growing concern. The ability to pickle a wide variety of fruits and vegetables also encourages the use of entire harvests, including parts of produce that might otherwise be thrown away, such as watermelon rinds or beet greens.

The practice of pickling also promotes sustainability through its low-energy preservation method. Unlike freezing or canning, pickling does not require continuous energy input to maintain the preserved state of the food. This characteristic makes pickling an eco-friendly alternative to other preservation techniques, aligning with efforts to reduce energy consumption and minimize environmental footprints. Furthermore, pickling utilizes simple, natural ingredients like salt, water, and vinegar, which are readily available and have minimal environmental impact compared to the production and disposal of synthetic preservatives.

Culturally, the benefits of pickling extend to the preservation of heritage and the fostering of community. Pickling recipes are often passed down through generations, serving as a tangible connection to cultural traditions and family histories. This aspect of pickling enriches the cultural tapestry of communities, offering a means to celebrate and share cultural identities through food. The communal nature of pickling, where friends and families come together to pickle the season's harvest, strengthens social bonds as well as encourages a sense of belonging and shared purpose.

In contemporary society, the resurgence of interest in pickling reflects a broader movement towards health-conscious, sustainable living. As individuals become more concious of the effect of their dietary decisions on their health and the environment, pickling emerges as a practical and beneficial practice. It offers a way to enjoy the bounty of each season throughout the year, reduce dependence on industrially processed foods, and embrace a more holistic approach to nutrition and wellness.

In conclusion, the benefits of pickling extend far beyond the mere preservation of food. This time-honored practice contributes to improved health through enhanced nutritional value and probiotic content, adds depth and variety to culinary traditions, addresses environmental concerns by reducing food waste and energy consumption, and preserves cultural heritage. As society grapples with the challenges of sustainable living and healthful eating, pickling stands out as a valuable and versatile solution, embodying the intersection of tradition, innovation, and sustainability.

Basic principles of pickling

Pickling, an ancient culinary practice, embodies a confluence of science, tradition, and art, offering a fascinating glimpse into the human quest for preservation, flavor, and health. This technique, deeply rooted in our historical and cultural landscapes, utilizes the transformative powers of acidification to extend the shelf life of foods, while imbuing them with unique flavors and textures. The basic principles of pickling are underpinned by the interaction of salt, acid, and the natural microbiome of foods, creating an environment where freshness is preserved, and spoilage is kept at bay. This section delves into the foundational concepts of pickling, exploring the scientific mechanisms at play and the critical elements that ensure its success.

At the heart of pickling lies the principle of acidification, which is pivotal in preventing the growth of harmful microorganisms. This acidic environment can be achieved through the addition of vinegar (acetic acid) or through the natural fermentation process, where salt encourages the growth of beneficial bacteria that produce lactic acid. The choice between these two methods—vinegar-based pickling or fermentation—dictates the final product's flavor, texture, and nutritional properties. Vinegar-based pickling, characterized by its immediate acidification, has a tangy flavor profile and a crisp texture, making it ideal for fruits and vegetables for short-term consumption. Fermentation, on the other hand, is a slower process that not only preserves but also enhances the nutritional value of foods, introducing probiotics and increasing vitamin content, particularly B vitamins.

The role of salt in pickling cannot be overstated. In fermentation, salt is essential for drawing water out of the produce, creating a brine where beneficial lactobacilli can thrive, outcompeting harmful bacteria. This brine is a protective barrier against spoilage, ensuring the safety and longevity of the pickled items. Salt concentration is meticulously calibrated to balance preservation needs with flavor, underscoring the precision required in successful pickling endeavors.

Temperature and time are also critical factors in the pickling process. Fermentation requires a controlled environment where temperature is carefully monitored to optimize the activity of beneficial bacteria without inviting spoilage organisms or hindering the fermentation process. The duration of fermentation varies, influencing the depth of flavor, acidity, and texture of the pickled product. This temporal aspect of pickling speaks to the patience and observation skills necessary to master the art, allowing the natural progression of flavors to unfold.

Hygiene and cleanliness are paramount in pickling, as introducing unwanted bacteria or contaminants can spoil the food and pose health risks. Utensils, containers, and produce must be thoroughly cleaned to ensure a successful and safe pickling process. This principle of meticulous cleanliness connects the practice of pickling to broader themes of health and safety in food preparation.

Beyond these technical aspects, pickling embodies a principle of sustainability and resourcefulness. It allows for preserving seasonal produce, reducing waste and ensuring a supply of nutritious foods throughout the year. This aspect of pickling resonates with contemporary concerns around food security and environmental stewardship, highlighting the relevance of this ancient practice in today's world.

Culturally, pickling serves as a canvas for creativity and tradition, allowing for the infusion of local flavors, spices, and herbs. This principle of cultural expression enriches the pickling process, reflecting the diverse culinary landscapes from which it emerges. From the spicy kimchi of Korea to the dill-laden pickles of Eastern Europe, pickling is a testament to people's ingenuity and cultural heritage worldwide.

In summary, the basic principles of pickling—acidification, the role of salt, temperature and time management, cleanliness, sustainability, and cultural expression—form the foundation of this time-honored practice. These principles guide the transformation of perishable produce into preserved delicacies, ensuring safety, enhancing flavors, and enriching our diets. Pickling stands as a bridge between past and present, a culinary art that continues to evolve while remaining deeply rooted in the wisdom of our ancestors. As we embrace the science and tradition of pickling, we not only preserve food but also the cultural and nutritional legacies that nourish future generations.

Equipment and tools needed for pickling

The art of pickling, an age-old method of preserving food, is a culinary tradition and a bridge to the past, connecting us to generations of knowledge and culture. While the essence of pickling lies in its simplicity and accessibility, the process requires specific equipment and tools to ensure success and safety. This section explores the essential equipment and tools needed for pickling, emphasizing their role in the preservation process and how they contribute to creating flavorful, safe, and high- quality pickled goods.

At the heart of the pickling process is the container used to hold the produce and pickling medium. Glass jars, particularly mason jars, are the most popular choice for home pickling due to their non-reactive nature, durability, and the airtight seal provided by their two-part lids, consisting of a flat disk and a screw band. The non-reactive nature of glass ensures that it does not interact chemically with the acidic pickling solution, thereby preserving the taste and safety of the pickled products.

Additionally, the transparency of glass jars allows for easy monitoring of the pickling process, enabling picklers to visually inspect their creations for signs of spoilage or fermentation activity.

Another crucial tool in the pickler's arsenal is a wide-mouth funnel. This simple yet effective tool facilitates the clean and efficient transfer of produce and brine into jars, minimizing spills and ensuring a tidy workspace. The wide mouth of the funnel is particularly useful when working with chunky vegetables or fruits, allowing for smooth passage into jars.

Accurate measurement tools are indispensable to achieve the precise balance of flavors that characterizes good pickles. Measuring cups and spoons are crucial for measuring water, vinegar, salt, sugar, and spices according to recipe specifications. Precision in measurement ensures the correct proportion of acidity, saltiness, and sweetness, which is critical for both the flavor profile and the safety of the pickled products.

The pickling process often involves heating the pickling brine to dissolve salt and sugar and to infuse the liquid with flavors from spices and herbs. A large, non-reactive pot is necessary for this task. Stainless steel or enameled pots are preferred as they do not react with acidic ingredients. This pot serves multiple purposes, from preparing the brine to water bath canning, a process used to create a vacuum seal on jars for long-term storage.

Tongs and jar lifters are vital for safely handling hot jars and lids during the canning process. Jar lifters, specially designed to grip the rims of mason jars, allow for the secure transfer of filled jars into and out of boiling water baths without risk of burns or jar breakage. Similarly, magnetic lid lifters are handy tools for placing sterilized lids onto jars, minimizing the risk of contamination.

Creating an airtight seal is crucial for preserving pickled goods' shelf life and safety. A headspace tool, which may also function as a bubble remover, is a simple device used to ensure the proper amount of space between the top of the food or liquid and also on the rim of the jar. This space is necessary to expand the contents during the heat processing stage and create a vacuum seal as the jars cool. The bubble remover end of the tool is used to gently stir the contents, releasing trapped air bubbles, which can affect the final product's sealing process and quality.

For those practicing fermentation-based pickling, such as making sauerkraut or kimchi, additional equipment, such as fermentation weights and airlocks, may be required. Fermentation weights are used to submerge the produce in brine, preventing exposure to air, which can lead to mold growth. Airlocks, fitted to the lids of fermentation containers, allow gases developed during fermentation to escape while preventing outside air from entering, creating an anaerobic environment conducive to fermentation.

Lastly, cleanliness and sterilization are paramount in pickling to prevent foodborne illnesses. This requires using non-abrasive cleaners and sanitizers suitable for food contact surfaces, including the jars, lids, and all tools used in the process. Sterilizing equipment before use, either by boiling or using a dishwasher with a sanitizing cycle, ensures that the pickling process starts with a clean slate, minimizing the risk of contamination.

In conclusion, while the act of pickling may seem straightforward, the quality and safety of the final product depend heavily on the proper selection and use of specific equipment and tools. From glass jars to fermentation weights, each tool are critical in guaranteeing the success of the pickling process. By understanding and assembling the right equipment, enthusiasts can confidently embark on their pickling journey, preserving not only food but also a piece of culinary heritage.

Common ingredients used in pickling

Pickling, a culinary art with ancient roots, involves preserving a variety of foods by immersing them in a solution of vinegar or saltwater brine, often with the addition of spices and herbs. This process extends the shelf life of perishable items and transforms their flavors, textures, and nutritional profiles. The choice of ingredients used in pickling is vast as well as varied, reflecting the rich tapestry of global food cultures and traditions. This section delves into the common ingredients found in pickling recipes, exploring their roles and how they contribute to the unique characteristics of pickled products.

The base liquids are at the foundation of any pickling process: vinegar and brine. Vinegar, a versatile pickling agent, is acidic enough to create an environment that prevents bacterial growth. It comes in various forms, including apple cider vinegar, known for its fruity undertones; white vinegar, prized for its neutrality; and specialty vinegars like balsamic or rice vinegar, each adding their distinct flavors to the pickled goods. The alternative to vinegar, a saltwater brine, relies on fermentation to produce the acidic conditions necessary for preservation. The salt in the brine brings out moisture from the produce, creating an environment where beneficial bacteria thrive, producing lactic acid as a byproduct. This method is often used for fermenting vegetables like cucumbers into pickles or cabbage into sauerkraut.

Water is another critical ingredient, serving as the medium to dissolve salt or vinegar to create the pickling solution. The purity of the water is essential, as impurities can affect the flavor and safety of the pickled product. Distilled or filtered water is often recommended to make sure that the final product is safe to consume and it is of the highest quality in terms of taste and appearance.

Salt is indispensable in pickling, acting as a preservative and flavoring agent. In fermentation-based pickling, salt inhibits the growth of harmful bacteria while allowing beneficial lactobacilli to thrive. The type of salt used can vary, with non-iodized salts like kosher salt or pickling salt preferred due to their lack of additives, which can interfere with the pickling process.

Sugar, while not required, is a common addition to many pickling recipes. It balances the acidity of the vinegar, adds complexity to the flavor profile, and can help retain the texture of the pickled item. The amount of sugar can be changed based on personal taste or the specific recipe being used.

Spices and herbs are the soul of pickling, infusing preserved foods with aromatic flavors and fragrances.

Common spices include mustard seeds, peppercorns, and dill seeds, each contributing its unique taste to the pickled concoction. Herbs such as dill, bay leaves, and garlic are also frequently used, offering depth and character to the final product. The combination of spices and herbs used in pickling is limited only by the imagination, allowing for endless customization and experimentation.

The main stars of any pickling endeavor are, of course, the fruits and vegetables themselves. Cucumbers, carrots, onions, and beets are popular choices, beloved for their crisp textures and ability to absorb the flavors of the pickling brine. Fruits like apples, pears, and cherries can also be pickled, resulting in sweet, tangy, and spicy treats that defy traditional flavor boundaries. Additionally, more adventurous picklers might experiment with pickling eggs, meats, and even fish, expanding the realm of pickling beyond its vegetarian origins.

The acidity level, an often-overlooked ingredient, is crucial for ensuring the safety of pickled foods. The pH of the pickling solution must be low enough (typically a pH of 4.6 or lower) to prevent the growth of botulism bacteria. This is where the type and concentration of vinegar and the fermentation process play critical roles in creating a safe and stable product.

In conclusion, the common ingredients used in pickling are much more than mere components; they are the building blocks of a culinary tradition that spans millennia and cultures. From the base liquids of vinegar and brine to the spices, herbs, and produce that imbue pickled goods with their distinctive flavors and aromas, each ingredient are pivotal in the art and science of pickling. This process of preservation not only extends the life of foods but also enhances their taste, nutrition, and cultural significance, demonstrating the enduring appeal and versatility of pickling in cuisines worldwide.

Safety precautions when pickling

Pickling is known as an ancient method of food preservation that prolongs the shelf life of perishable foods and enhances their flavors and nutritional value. While the process of pickling can be rewarding and produce delicious results, it is crucial to follow specific safety precautions to ensure that the pickled goods are safe to eat. This section will explore the safety precautions necessary when engaging in the pickling process, focusing on the importance of cleanliness, proper ingredients and equipment use, and adherence to tested recipes and procedures.

Cleanliness is paramount in the pickling process. The environment in which pickling occurs, including the work surfaces, equipment, and the hands of the person doing the pickling, must be thoroughly cleaned and sanitized. This step is critical to prevent the introduction of harmful bacteria or mold into the pickling jars, which could compromise the safety of the pickled products. Using hot, soapy water then performing a rinse and an appropriate food-safe sanitizer can effectively reduce the risk of contamination. All utensils, cutting boards, and containers used in the pickling process should be washed and sanitized before each use.

The choice of ingredients is another crucial aspect of safe pickling. Fresh, high-quality produce free of bruises and blemishes should be used, as damaged areas can harbor bacteria that might lead to spoilage. When selecting vinegar for pickling, it is essential to use types with sufficient acidity, typically with an acetic acid concentration of 5% at least. This level of acidity is necessary to inhibit the growth of harmful bacteria, including Clostridium botulinum, which can cause botulism, a potentially fatal illness. Similarly, when salt is required, especially in fermentation-based pickling, using non-iodized salt without anti-caking agents is advisable, as these additives can interfere with fermentation.

Proper equipment is also vital for safe pickling. Glass jars with tight-fitting lids are commonly used because they do not react with acidic ingredients. Before use, jars and lids should be inspected for cracks, chips, or rust, which could compromise the seal or introduce contaminants. Sterilizing jars and lids by boiling them in water for a specified time or using a dishwasher with a sterilization feature is recommended to eliminate any pathogens present.

Adherence to tested and trusted recipes is another essential safety precaution. While experimentation is a natural part of the culinary experience, deviating from established pickling recipes can lead to unsafe acidity levels, compromising the safety of the finished product. Tested recipes provide specific ratios of vinegar, water, and salt necessary to achieve a safe pH level, typically below 4.6, preventing harmful microorganisms' growth. Furthermore, following the processing times and methods recommended in the recipe ensures that the pickles are properly preserved and safe to consume.

Monitoring the fermentation process, when applicable, is critical to ensure safety. Signs of successful fermentation include bubbles in the brine, a sour smell, and a cloudy appearance of the liquid, indicating the activity of beneficial lactic acid bacteria. However, the presence of mold, off-odors, or a slimy texture indicates spoilage, and such batches should be discarded. It is essential to keep the fermenting vegetables submerged under the brine to prevent exposure to air, which can lead to mold development and spoilage.

Finally, storing pickled products correctly is a key safety measure. Once jars are sealed, they should be stored in a cool, dark place and regularly checked for signs of spoilage, such as leaking, gas bubbles, or bulging lids.

Refrigeration is required for some types of pickles, especially those made with a lower concentration of vinegar or those that are fermented, to slow down fermentation and maintain safety and quality.

In conclusion, while pickling is a rewarding process that can yield delicious and nutritious preserved foods, it is imperative to follow safety precautions meticulously. Cleanliness, the use of proper ingredients and equipment, adherence to tested recipes, monitoring the fermentation process, and correct storage are all crucial steps in ensuring the safety of pickled products. By taking these precautions, enthusiasts can confidently enjoy the fruits of their labor, knowing that their pickled goods are not only tasty but also safe to consume.

CHAPTER III

Pickling Techniques

Traditional pickling methods

Traditional pickling methods have been a cornerstone of food preservation and culinary traditions worldwide for thousands of years. These techniques, passed down through generations, have allowed communities to store seasonal produce for consumption throughout the year, enhancing both their diets' flavor and nutritional value. This section explores various traditional pickling methods, shedding light on the cultural significance and diversity of practices that have stood the test of time.

Fundamentally, pickling is the practice of preserving food through immersion in vinegar or anaerobic fermentation in brine. This method of preservation leverages the natural fermentation process or the acidity of vinegar to inhibit bacterial growth that causes food spoilage. While the basic principles of pickling remain consistent, traditional methods vary widely among different cultures, each adding its unique twist to the process.

One of the oldest and most widespread methods of traditional pickling is through lacto-fermentation. This process involves submerging vegetables in a brine solution made from water and salt. The salt concentration is critical; it must be enough to inhibit the development of harmful bacteria while allowing the proliferation of Lactobacillus bacteria, naturally present on the surface of vegetables. As these bacteria metabolize the sugars in the vegetables, they produce lactic acid, which acts as a natural preservative. This method is responsible for creating classics such as sauerkraut in Germany, kimchi in Korea, and dill pickles in various Eastern European cultures. Lacto-fermented pickles are not only cherished for their tangy taste but also for their health benefits, including improved digestion and enhanced gut health due to the presence of probiotics.

Another traditional method involves using vinegar, a powerful antimicrobial agent, to pickle foods. Unlike lacto-fermentation, vinegar pickling does not necessarily involve fermentation and can preserve a broader range of foods, including fruits, meats, and eggs. The acidic environment created by the vinegar halts the growth of spoilage-causing microorganisms. In addition to preservation, vinegar imparts a distinct sharpness to the pickled items, which can be further flavored with herbs, spices, and sweeteners. British pickled onions, Indian mango pickle (achar), and American bread-and-butter pickles exemplify the diversity of vinegar-based pickling traditions.

A notable variation of traditional pickling is found in the Japanese method of tsukemono, which includes a variety of techniques such as shiozuke (salt pickling), misozuke (miso pickling), and shoyuzuke (soy sauce pickling). These methods utilize different agents for both flavor and preservation, showcasing the adaptability of pickling practices to local tastes and available ingredients. Similarly, in the Middle East and the Mediterranean, pickled foods like lemons and olives are integral to the culinary landscape, preserved using methods that have been refined over centuries.

The cultural significance of traditional pickling methods extends beyond mere food preservation. These practices are deeply entwined with the agricultural calendar, religious traditions, and family gatherings. Pickling seasons are often communal events, where families and neighbors come together to process the harvest, sharing recipes, techniques, and stories. This communal aspect of pickling strengthens social bonds and passes down culinary heritage through generations.

Despite the advent of modern refrigeration and food preservation technologies, traditional pickling methods continue to enjoy popularity and reverence. This resurgence can be attributed to a expanding appreciation for artisanal foods, the desire for natural fermentation's health benefits, and an interest in sustainable living practices. Furthermore, the global exchange of culinary traditions through travel and communication has led to a cross-pollination of pickling techniques, introducing new flavors and methods to different cultures.

In conclusion, traditional pickling methods are a testament to human ingenuity in food preservation. These techniques have not only enabled generations to store and enjoy seasonal produce year-round but have also enriched our culinary traditions with a tapestry of flavors and textures. The diversity of pickling practices across cultures highlights the adaptability and creativity of communities in making the most of their local resources. As we continue to explore and embrace these traditional methods, we not only preserve a piece of culinary heritage but also contribute to a sustainable and health-conscious food culture.

Quick pickling techniques

Quick pickling, also known as refrigerator pickling, has emerged as a popular and accessible method for preserving various foods without the need for the lengthy fermentation process or canning techniques associated with traditional pickling. This method allows for the rapid infusion of flavors and the extension of the shelf life of perishable items, making it an appealing option for home cooks looking to add zest and tang to their meals with minimal effort. This section explores quick pickling techniques, their benefits, and how they distinguish themselves from more time-honored pickling methods.

At its core, quick pickling involves submerging raw or briefly blanched vegetables and fruits in a vinegar-based brine, often flavored with salt, sugar, and an assortment of herbs and spices. The acid from the vinegar acts as a preservative, inhibiting the growth of bacteria that cause food to spoil, while the added flavors transform the produce into a deliciously tangy accompaniment to a wide range of dishes. Unlike traditional pickling, which can take weeks or even months to reach the desired flavor and preservation level, quick pickling can produce ready-to-eat pickles in as little as a few hours.

The process of quick pickling begins with choosing the right produce. Fresh, crisp vegetables and fruits are essential for achieving the best texture and flavor. Common choices include cucumbers, carrots, radishes, onions, and green beans, but virtually any vegetable or firm fruit can be quick pickled. The produce is then cleaned and cut into the desired shapes and sizes, such as slices, spears, or rings, to allow for even flavor absorption.

The next step entails preparing the pickling brine, which typically consists of vinegar, water, salt, and sugar. While white vinegar is a well-known choice due to its clear color and neutral flavor, other vinegars like apple cider, red wine, or rice vinegar can be used to impart different tastes. The proportions of salt as well as sugar can be adjusted depending on personal preference, with more sugar yielding a sweeter pickle and more salt producing a saltier one. The brine is brought to a boil, ensuring the salt as well as sugar are completely dissolved, and then allowed to cool slightly prior being poured over the prepared produce.

To customize the pickles' flavor profile, various herbs, spices, and aromatics can be added to the jars before filling them with the produce and brine. Common additions include garlic cloves, dill sprigs, mustard seeds, peppercorns, and red pepper flakes, but the possibilities are limited only by the imagination of the cook. Combining these flavors with the vinegar brine creates a complex and delightful taste experience that enhances the natural flavors of the pickled items.

Once the jars are filled and sealed, they are refrigerated for at least a few hours, though the flavors will continue to develop and deepen over the following days. Quick pickles are typically ready to eat within 24 hours and can be kept in the refrigerator for up to a month, offering a convenient and delicious way to enjoy preserved produce without the lengthy wait associated with traditional methods.

Quick pickling techniques offer several advantages beyond their simplicity and speed. They let cooks to experiment with different flavor combinations and to make small batches of pickles without the commitment required for larger-scale canning projects. Moreover, quick pickling can be an excellent way to mitigate food waste by preserving excess produce that might otherwise spoil.

However, it is essential to note that quick pickles are not intended for long-term storage outside of refrigeration. The method does not involve the sterilization process required for shelf-stable canned goods, so quick pickles must be kept refrigerated and consumed relatively quickly.

In conclusion, quick pickling techniques provide a fast, easy, and versatile method for preserving and enhancing the flavors of various produce. By combining vinegar with salt, sugar, herbs, and spices, home cooks can create an endless variety of tangy, flavorful pickles in just a fraction of the time required by traditional methods. Whether used as a garnish, a snack, or a component of a larger dish, quick pickles add a vibrant touch to any meal, showcasing the art of pickling in its most accessible form. As interest in homemade and artisanal foods grows, quick pickling stands out as a simple yet satisfying way to explore the joys of culinary preservation.

Fermentation vs. vinegar pickling

Preserving food through pickling is a practice as ancient as civilization, embodying a rich diversity of techniques and traditions. Two primary methods stand at the forefront of this culinary art: fermentation and vinegar pickling. Each technique offers a unique approach to extending the shelf life of food, enhancing its flavors, and boosting its nutritional value. This section explores the differences between fermentation and vinegar pickling, delving into the science behind these practices, their historical roots, and their impacts on taste and health.

Fermentation is known as a metabolic process that produces chemical changes in organic substrates through the action of enzymes. In pickling, fermentation refers to transforming sugars in vegetables and fruits into lactic acid by beneficial bacteria, predominantly from the Lactobacillus species. This lactic acid prevents the growth of dangerous bacteria, acting as a natural preservative. Fermented pickles, such as sauerkraut, kimchi, and traditional dill pickles, are not just preserved by this acid; they are also enriched with probiotics, vitamins, and enzymes. The process typically begins with submerging the produce in a brine solution of salt and water, establishing an anaerobic environment that encourages the growth of these beneficial bacteria. Over days to weeks, the vegetables ferment, developing complex, tangy flavors and a crisp texture.

Vinegar pickling, by contrast, involves immersing foods in a solution of vinegar, water, and often salt and sugar, along with various spices and herbs for flavor. Vinegar, an acidic liquid, serves as the preservative in this method, creating an inhospitable environment to spoilage-causing microbes. Unlike fermentation, vinegar pickling does not significantly alter the nutritional content of the food, nor does it introduce probiotics. However, it does offer a quicker, more predictable process, with pickles ready to eat in a matter of days. The sharp, piquant flavor of vinegar-pickled foods is distinctive, ranging from the sweet-and-sour profiles of bread and butter pickles to the robust spice of pickled jalapenos.

Historically, both methods have deep cultural roots, evolving from the need to preserve the bounty of harvests for leaner times. Fermentation is recognized as one of the oldest food preservation techniques, with evidence of fermented foods dating back thousands of years in Chinese, Egyptian, and Roman cultures, among others.

These traditions have been passed down through generations, adapting to local tastes and available ingredients. Vinegar pickling also has a storied history, with vinegar being used as a preservative since ancient times. Its application in pickling became more widespread with the advent of mass-produced vinegar in the 19th century, making it an accessible option for home cooks.

The choice between fermentation and vinegar pickling often comes down to the desired outcome regarding flavor, texture, and health benefits. Fermentation can yield a greater depth of flavor and a crunchier texture, along with the added benefits of probiotics, which are known to support gut health. The slow, natural process of fermentation also allows for a more nuanced development of flavors, with each batch varying slightly based on factors such as temperature, salt concentration, and the specific strains of bacteria present.

Vinegar pickling, on the other hand, offers consistency and control, with the vinegar's acidic environment ensuring a uniform taste and preservation across batches. This method can also accommodate a wider variety of spices and flavorings, allowing for greater creativity in the pickling process. However, it lacks the probiotic benefits of fermented pickles and can result in a softer texture if the produce is left in the acidic solution for too long.

Both methods offer advantages in terms of health considerations. Fermented foods take part to a healthy gut microbiome, which is linked to enhanced digestion, immunity, and even mental health. Apple cider vinegar in particular has been promoted for its possible health benefits, which include heart health and blood sugar management. However, these benefits are more associated with vinegar itself than vinegar-pickled foods.

In conclusion, fermentation and vinegar pickling represent two distinct paths within the art of pickling, each with its unique processes, flavors, and health benefits. Fermentation offers a window into the ancient practices of food preservation, bringing with it the benefits of probiotics and complex flavors. Vinegar pickling provides a more immediate gratification, with its sharp tang and endless variety of flavor infusions. Both methods underscore the ingenuity of human culinary traditions, offering delicious and healthful ways to enjoy the harvest's bounty throughout the year. As we continue to explore and embrace these techniques, we preserve food and the rich cultural heritage embedded in the art of pickling.

Troubleshooting common pickling problems

With its ancient roots and diverse cultural expressions, the art of pickling remains a widespread culinary practice for preserving food. While the process can be straightforward and rewarding, novice and experienced picklers may encounter issues affecting the quality, safety, and taste of their pickled products. This section explores common pickling problems, offering solutions and tips for troubleshooting these challenges, ensuring the success and enjoyment of home pickling endeavors.

One frequent issue faced by home picklers is the softening or loss of crispness in pickled vegetables. The hallmark of a great pickle is its crunch, but various factors can compromise this desired texture. One common culprit is the use of iodized salt, which can interfere with the firmness of vegetables. To prevent softening, it is advisable to use pickling salt or kosher salt, both of which are free from additives that can cause vegetables to become mushy. Another factor is the freshness of the produce; vegetables should be pickled soon after harvest for optimal crispness. Additionally, the inclusion of tannin-rich leaves, such as grape, oak, or horseradish leaves, in the pickling jar can help maintain crispness by inhibiting enzymes that soften the vegetables.

Another issue often encountered in pickling is cloudiness in the brine, which can be unsettling and raise concerns about spoilage. While a cloudy brine can result from harmless starches the vegetables release, it can also indicate microbial growth. Ensuring the cleanliness of all equipment and produce before starting the pickling process can minimize this risk. If fermentation is the goal, a certain degree of cloudiness is natural and expected as beneficial bacteria proliferate. However, if the cloudiness is accompanied by off odors, sliminess, or mold, it is best to discard the batch to avoid possible health risks.

Discoloration of pickles or the pickling liquid can also occur, detracting from the visual appeal of the final product. Factors contributing to discoloration include the use of tap water with high iron content, which can react with the pickling process, and the presence of minerals in natural salts. Using distilled water and pickling salt can mitigate these issues. Additionally, exposure to light can cause fading or color changes in pickles; storing jars in a cool, dark place can help preserve their color.

Mold growth is a concerning problem that can arise during pickling, especially in fermented pickles. Mold can develop if the vegetables are not fully submerged under the brine, exposing them to air. Using a fermentation weight to submerge the produce and ensuring a tight seal on the container can prevent mold growth. If mold appears on the surface of the brine, it may be possible to remove it and salvage the ferment, provided the mold has not penetrated the brine. However, if there is any doubt about the product's safety, discarding it is safer.

Failure to achieve a proper seal on jars during the canning process can compromise the shelf stability of vinegar pickles. A faulty seal can allow air to enter the jar, leading to spoilage. Ensuring that jar rims are clean and debris-free before applying lids, using new lids for each batch, and following recommended canning procedures can improve seal success rates. After processing, checking that lids have properly sealed by pressing down on the center of the lid (it should not pop back) can identify any sealing failures.

Lastly, an imbalance in flavor—whether too salty, too sweet, or too acidic—is a common issue that can usually be adjusted in future batches by modifying the ratios of salt, sugar, and vinegar in the pickling solution. Keeping detailed notes on adjustments made to recipes can help refine the pickler's craft over time, leading to personalized and perfected pickle flavors.

In conclusion, while pickling is a rewarding practice that connects us to our culinary heritage and offers a means of preserving food, it is not without its challenges. Understanding the common problems that can arise during pickling and knowing how to troubleshoot them can significantly enhance the pickling experience. By paying close attention to the quality of ingredients, the cleanliness of equipment, and the specific steps of the pickling process, enthusiasts can produce delicious, safe, and crisp pickles that are a testament to the timeless art of pickling.

Creative flavor combinations for pickling

Pickling, a culinary practice rooted in the necessity of preservation, has evolved into an art form that allows for endless creativity and innovation in the kitchen. Beyond the traditional dill cucumber pickle, a world of flavor combinations is waiting to be explored, each offering a unique twist on classic techniques. This section delves into the realm of creative flavor combinations for pickling, highlighting how mixing various spices, herbs, fruits, and vegetables can elevate the humble pickle into a gourmet delight.

At the heart of creative pickling is the adventurous spirit of combining unexpected flavors to create something unique. One such example is the fusion of sweet and spicy elements, a pairing that appeals to those who crave complexity in their palate. Imagine the surprise and delight of tasting a pickled peach with a hint of habanero pepper. The natural sweetness of the peach contrasts beautifully with the habanero's fiery kick, creating a refreshing and invigorating pickle. This combination can be achieved by adding slices of habanero peppers to a brine of white vinegar, sugar, as well as a pinch of salt, then pouring it over fresh peach slices. The result is a tantalizing treat that pairs wonderfully with creamy cheeses or as a vibrant addition to salads.

Another avenue for exploration is incorporating aromatic herbs and floral notes into pickles. A prime example of this is lavender-infused pickled carrots. By adding a few sprigs of lavender to the pickling solution, along with traditional pickling spices like mustard seeds and peppercorns, the carrots are imbued with a subtle floral aroma that complements their natural sweetness. This innovative pairing not only adds depth to the flavor profile of the pickles but also introduces a touch of elegance, making them a sophisticated accompaniment to charcuterie boards or an unexpected twist to a roasted vegetable dish.

For those inclined towards the tangy and tart spectrum of flavors, combining citrus with root vegetables offers a refreshing take on pickled goods. Lemon and dill pickled beets are a stellar representation of this category. The bright acidity of the lemon pairs exquisitely with the earthiness of the beets, while dill adds freshness to the mix. The brine for this combination could include lemon zest and juice, white vinegar, a touch of sugar, salt, and generous amounts of fresh dill. This pickle is visually striking, with its vibrant hues and textures, and a flavorful powerhouse that can elevate simple salads or serve as a zesty side dish.

Exploring international flavor profiles opens up another dimension in creative pickling. Inspired by Asian cuisine, one can create a pickled daikon radish with ginger and star anise. This combination draws on the radish's crisp texture and mild flavor as a canvas for the warmth of ginger and the licorice-like notes of star anise. Such a pickle not only showcases the versatility of Asian spices but also serves as a deliciously crunchy and flavorful addition to rice dishes and salads or as a unique ingredient in sushi rolls.

Lastly, the marriage of fruit and heat offers an intriguing avenue for creative pickling. The pickled watermelon rind with jalapeño and lime is a standout in this category. This innovative pickle uses the often-discarded watermelon rind as a base, transforming it with the addition of lime zest and slices of jalapeño for a spicy kick. The combination of the cool, crisp rind with the zesty lime and the jalapeño heat results in a refreshing and spicy pickle, perfect for summer barbecues or as a bold garnish for cocktails.

In conclusion, the world of creative pickling is limited only by one's imagination. By stepping outside the bounds of traditional flavor combinations and experimenting with sweet, spicy, floral, tangy, and international ingredients, one can transform the simple act of pickling into an art form. These inventive flavor pairings not only enhance the taste and appeal of pickled foods but also encourage culinary experimentation and discovery. As more individuals embrace the creativity that pickling offers, the tradition continues to evolve, enriching our culinary heritage with each new and unexpected combination.

CHAPTER IV

Fermentation Fundamentals

What is fermentation?

Sugar can be metabolically fermented to produce acids, gases, or alcohol. It happens in bacteria, yeast, and muscle cells that are oxygen-starved, as in the case of lactic acid fermentation. Zymology is the scientific study of fermentation. Food has been preserved through this process for thousands of years, and alcoholic beverages have been made with it. More recently, fermented foods have been linked to health benefits. This section delves into the intricacies of fermentation, exploring its biological mechanisms, historical significance, and the diverse applications that make it a cornerstone of culinary and biochemical processes.

At its core, fermentation is an anaerobic process, meaning it takes place without oxygen. The most prevalent type of fermentation occurs when yeast converts carbohydrates to alcohol and carbon dioxide, a process that underpins the production of beer, wine, and spirits. In this process, yeast cells consume sugar and convert it into alcohol and carbon dioxide, generating energy for their own growth and reproduction. This transformation not only produces alcoholic beverages but also causes dough to rise, thanks to the carbon dioxide released during fermentation.

Lactobacilli and other bacteria convert sugar into lactic acid during lactic acid fermentation, another form of fermentation. This form of fermentation is responsible for the sour taste of yogurt, the tang of sauerkraut, and the flavor of other fermented foods like kimchi, kefir, and sourdough bread. Lactic acid fermentation not only extends the shelf life of these foods but also enhances their digestibility and nutritional profile. The process encourages the growth of beneficial bacteria, known as probiotics, which contribute to gut health and overall well- being.

The historical significance of fermentation cannot be overstated. Evidence of fermented beverages dates back to 7000 BC in what is now China, with similar discoveries in Georgia, Iran, and other parts of the world suggesting that fermentation has been a global practice for millennia. The food preservation through fermentation allowed ancient civilizations to store surplus produce, survive harsh winters, and transport food over long distances. Moreover, fermented foods played a vital role in the diets of our ancestors, providing essential nutrients and beneficial bacteria that likely contributed to their health and longevity.

Fermentation also holds a revered place in various cultural traditions, where it is intertwined with social, religious, and ceremonial practices. For example, wine has significant religious symbolism in Christianity, while fermented foods like kimchi are deeply embedded in Korean culture. These traditions highlight the cultural diversity of fermentation practices and their importance in culinary heritage across the globe.

In recent years, there has been a resurgence of interest in fermentation, driven by the growing awareness of the health benefits interconnected with fermented foods. Research has present that fermented foods can enhance digestion, boost immunity, and even mitigate the risk of certain diseases. This has led to a renewed appreciation for traditional fermentation techniques and an explosion of artisanal and home fermentation practices. People are experimenting with fermentation to create delicious foods and beverages and explore the health benefits of consuming probiotic-rich products.

Furthermore, fermentation has applications beyond food and beverage production. It is a crucial process in industrial biotechnology, where it is used to produce antibiotics, hormones, and vitamins, as well as biofuel. The versatility of fermentation as a biological process underscores its potential for sustainable practices and solutions to modern challenges.

In conclusion, fermentation is a fascinating and multifaceted process with deep historical roots and widespread cultural significance. It represents a convergence of science, tradition, and art, enabling the transformation of simple ingredients into complex flavors, textures, and health benefits. As we continue to explore and understand the mechanisms and impacts of fermentation, it is clear that this ancient practice will remain an integral part of human culture, cuisine, and innovation for generations to come. Whether for the preservation of food, the production of alcoholic beverages, or the cultivation of beneficial bacteria, fermentation continues to enrich our lives in myriad ways, highlighting the incredible potential of harnessing natural processes for human benefit.

Benefits of fermentation

Fermentation, an age-old biochemical process, has been harnessed by various cultures worldwide for thousands of years. This process, driven by microorganisms such as bacteria and yeast, transforms food to enhance its nutritional value, flavor, and shelf life. Beyond these practical applications, the benefits of fermentation extend to health and wellness, contributing to a balanced diet and supporting digestive health. This section explores the multifaceted benefits of fermentation, highlighting its impact on nutrition, health, culinary diversity, and environmental sustainability.

Nutritional enhancement stands out as one of the most significant benefits of fermentation. Through the fermentation process, the bioavailability of nutrients in food is often increased, making them easier for the body to absorb. For instance, fermentation can break down phytic acid, a compound found in grains and legumes that binds minerals and reduces their absorption. The reduction of phytic acid through fermentation allows for increased levels of minerals such as iron, zinc, and magnesium to be available for absorption. Additionally, fermentation can produce essential nutrients, including vitamins B and K and amino acids, enriching the nutritional profile of fermented foods.

Fermentation also plays a crucial role in enhancing gut health. Probiotics, also referred to as beneficial bacteria that colonize the digestive tract, are abundant in fermented foods. These probiotics contribute to the balance of gut flora, supporting the immune system and promoting healthy digestion. The fermented foods consumption has been associated to various health benefits, including improved digestion, alleviation of lactose intolerance symptoms, and even a reduced risk of certain chronic diseases. The probiotic content of fermented foods like yogurt, kefir, and sauerkraut supports the body's ability to fight infections and absorb nutrients, highlighting the integral role of gut health in overall well-being.

The preservation of food is another hallmark benefit of fermentation. Before the advent of modern refrigeration, fermentation served as a critical method for extending the shelf life of perishable items. By creating an acidic environment that hinders the growth of spoilage-causing microorganisms, fermentation ensures that foods remain safe and edible for more extended periods. This natural preservation method not only contributes to food security but also reduces waste by allowing for the storage of surplus produce. In today's context, fermentation continues to be valued for its sustainability, offering an eco-friendly alternative to energy-intensive refrigeration and food preservation techniques.

Fermentation contributes significantly to culinary diversity and gastronomy. The process imparts unique flavors, aromas, and textures to food, enriching culinary traditions around the globe. From the tangy complexity of kimchi in Korean cuisine to the sourdough bread's distinctive taste, fermentation introduces an array of flavors that cannot be replicated through other cooking methods. These fermented foods enhance the sensory experience of eating and celebrate cultural heritage, passing down recipes and techniques through generations. The global interest in fermented foods has spurred culinary innovation, encouraging chefs and home cooks alike to experiment with fermentation, discovering new flavors and reinvigorating traditional dishes.

Environmental sustainability is a further benefit of fermentation, particularly relevant in the context of contemporary concerns about food production and waste. Fermentation processes often require minimal energy input and can utilize parts of food that might otherwise be discarded. For example, pickling can transform surplus vegetables into a delicious and long-lasting product, while the fermentation of grains and dairy contributes to efficiently using these resources. By reducing reliance on refrigeration and minimizing food waste, fermentation practices contribute to more sustainable food systems, highlighting the interconnectedness of culinary practices and environmental stewardship.

In conclusion, the benefits of fermentation are vast and varied, encompassing nutritional enhancement, gut health, food preservation, culinary diversity, and environmental sustainability. This ancient practice, rooted in the natural world's biological processes, offers modern solutions to contemporary challenges, from improving health outcomes to addressing food security and sustainability. As awareness of these benefits grows, so does the appreciation for fermented foods, not only as a means of preservation but as a cornerstone of a healthy, diverse, and sustainable diet. Fermentation embodies the synthesis of tradition and innovation, providing a tangible link between the past and present while offering promising avenues for future exploration in nutrition, gastronomy, and environmental sustainability.

Basic principles of fermentation

Fermentation is a remarkable biological process that harnesses the power of microorganisms to transform food and beverages. This ancient practice, which predates recorded history, is critical in food preservation, health, and culture. The basic principles of fermentation are grounded in microbiology and chemistry, involving the metabolic conversion of sugars into alcohol, gases, or organic acids under anaerobic conditions. Understanding these foundational principles not only demystifies the process but also reveals the science behind fermented products' flavors, textures, and nutritional benefits.

At its core, fermentation is an energy-releasing process that occurs in the absence of oxygen. It involves various microorganisms, including bacteria, yeasts, and molds, each playing a distinct role in transforming substrates—usually carbohydrates—into other compounds. These microorganisms are the true artisans of fermentation, with each species contributing its unique metabolic pathways to produce a diverse array of fermented foods and drinks enjoyed worldwide.

The most common type of fermentation is lactic acid fermentation, in which lactic acid bacteria (LAB) convert sugars into lactic acid. This process is responsible for the sour taste of yogurt, sauerkraut, and kimchi. LAB are facultative anaerobes, meaning they can operate in both the presence and absence of oxygen, but prefer anaerobic conditions for lactic acid production. The acidity generated by lactic acid not only preserves the food by inhibiting the development of harmful bacteria but also promotes the digestion and absorption of nutrients.

Alcoholic fermentation, another widespread form of fermentation, is primarily conducted by yeasts, particularly Saccharomyces cerevisiae. In this process, yeasts metabolize sugars to produce ethanol and carbon dioxide. Alcoholic fermentation is the foundation of beer, wine, and spirits production. The carbon dioxide produced during fermentation is also what causes bread to rise, showcasing the versatility of fermentation applications.

Acetic acid fermentation is a two-step process involving the conversion of sugars to alcohol through yeast fermentation followed by the oxidation of alcohol to acetic acid by acetic acid bacteria. This process gives vinegar its characteristic sour taste and acidity. Unlike lactic acid and alcoholic fermentations, acetic acid fermentation requires oxygen, as it involves an aerobic transformation of ethanol into acetic acid.

The environment in which fermentation occurs is crucial to the success of the process. Factors such as temperature, pH, salinity, and the presence of oxygen must be carefully controlled to favor the growth as well as metabolic activity of the desired microorganisms. For example, most lactic acid fermentation processes thrive at a temperature range between 20°C-30°C (68°F-86°F) and in slightly acidic conditions. Too high or too low temperatures can inhibit microbial activity or encourage the growth of spoilage organisms, respectively.

The substrate—the food being fermented—also plays a significant role in the fermentation process. The composition of the substrate, including its sugar, nutrient, and water content, can influence the final product's flavor, texture, and nutritional profile. For instance, the type of milk used in yogurt making (cow, goat, sheep) will affect the taste and texture of the yogurt due to differences in milk composition.

An essential principle of successful fermentation is hygiene. While fermentation relies on the activity of beneficial microorganisms, the process can be easily contaminated by harmful bacteria, yeasts, or molds if proper sanitary practices are not followed. Utensils, containers, and the fermentation environment must be kept clean to ensure a safe and successful fermentation process.

In summary, the basic principles of fermentation revolve around the controlled activity of specific microorganisms that metabolize sugars during the absence of oxygen to produce acids, gases, or alcohol. This biochemical process not only preserves food and enhances its flavors and nutritional value but also contributes to the diversity of human diets and culinary traditions. Understanding these principles offers valuable insights into the art and science of fermentation, allowing both novices and experienced practitioners to explore and innovate within this ancient culinary practice. Through fermentation, we harness the natural world's microbial bounty, transforming simple ingredients into complex, flavorful, and nutritious foods that celebrate the intersection of biology, chemistry, and culture.

Equipment and tools needed for fermentation

Fermentation, a process revered for its ability to transform and preserve food, relies not just on the fermenter's skill but also on specific equipment and tools. These tools, which have evolved from ancient practices to modern culinary arts, are essential for creating an environment where beneficial microorganisms can thrive, ensuring the success of the fermentation process. This section explores the various equipment and tools necessary for fermentation, highlighting their functions and importance in producing high-quality fermented products.

At the foundation of any fermentation setup is the fermentation vessel. The ingredients are mixed with culture starters in this container and left to ferment. The choice of vessel is crucial and varies depending on the type of fermentation. Glass jars, for instance, are famous for small-batch fermentation of vegetables and fruits due to their non-reactive nature, which ensures that no unwanted flavors are imparted to the food. Similarly, ceramic crocks are favored for larger batches, especially for fermenting sauerkraut or kimchi, as they offer excellent insulation and help maintain a stable fermentation environment. These containers must be food-grade and able to be sealed to protect the ferment from contamination and oxygen, which could inhibit the fermentation process or introduce harmful bacteria.

Airlocks and lids are indispensable in the world of fermentation. An airlock is a device that let gases produced during fermentation to escape while hindering outside air from entering the vessel. This is crucial for creating an anaerobic (oxygen-free) environment necessary for certain types of fermentation, such as alcohol fermentation. For fermentations that require occasional exposure to air, such as kombucha, a cloth cover secured with a rubber band can be used. This cover keeps contaminants out while allowing the ferment to breathe.

Weights are another essential tool, particularly for vegetable fermentation. Fermentation weights submerge the produce in its brine, ensuring even fermentation and preventing exposure to air, which can lead to mold growth. These weights can be made of glass, ceramic, or food-grade plastic, and they are available in various shapes and sizes to fit different containers.

A crucial aspect of successful fermentation is maintaining the correct temperature, as temperature fluctuations can affect the activity of fermenting bacteria. A kitchen thermometer is a simple yet effective tool for monitoring the temperature of the fermentation environment. For more sophisticated setups, especially when fermenting beverages like beer or wine, temperature control systems can be used to keep the ferment at an optimal temperature throughout the process.

pH meters or test strips are used to monitor the acidity level of the ferment, which is a critical parameter in many fermentation processes. The acidity level can influence the fermented product's flavor, texture, and safety. For instance, ensuring that sauerkraut reaches the correct pH level is essential for preventing the growth of harmful bacteria.

In addition to these specialized tools, several basic kitchen utensils play essential roles in preparing and handling ingredients for fermentation. Knives and cutting boards are needed for chopping vegetables, while mixing bowls are used for combining ingredients before they are placed in the fermentation vessel. Measuring cups and spoons ensure that the correct ratios of salt, sugar, and culture starters are used, which is critical for the fermentation process to proceed correctly.

Lastly, a culture incubator might be necessary for those venturing into the fermentation of dairy products, such as yogurt or kefir. This equipment maintains a consistent temperature that is conducive to the growth of the specific cultures needed for dairy fermentation. While many home fermenters use a warm spot in their kitchen or a low oven, dedicated incubators can provide more precise temperature control, resulting in a more consistent product.

In conclusion, while ancient, fermentation benefits greatly from modern tools and equipment designed to create the optimal conditions for microbial activity. From basic kitchen utensils to specialized fermentation vessels, weights, and temperature control devices, the right equipment is essential for anyone looking to explore the art and science of fermentation. These tools facilitate the fermentation process and contribute to the finished product's safety, quality, and flavor. As interest in fermentation continues to grow, both for its health benefits and culinary possibilities, having the proper equipment will enable enthusiasts to delve deeper into this fascinating and flavorful world.

Common ingredients used in fermentation

Fermentation, a transformative process cherished across cultures, hinges not only on the microscopic work of bacteria and yeast but also on selecting key ingredients. Often humble in their raw form, these ingredients undergo a metamorphosis that elevates their flavors, textures, and nutritional profiles. Understanding the common ingredients used in fermentation is essential for both novices and seasoned practitioners of this ancient culinary art. This section delves into the vital components that fuel the fermentation process, exploring how each contributes to creating a myriad of fermented foods and beverages that are integral to global cuisines.

At the foundation of almost every fermentation endeavor are carbohydrates. These are the fuel that microorganisms consume during fermentation, converting them into acids, gases, or alcohol. Sugars, found in fruits, honey, and certain vegetables, are readily fermentable carbohydrates often used in the production of alcoholic beverages, which include wine and mead, as well as in lacto-fermented fruits and vegetables. Starches, another form of carbohydrate found in grains and tubers, are typically broken down into simpler sugars through cooking or malting, a process that makes them accessible for fermentation in products like beer and spirits.

Water is another critical ingredient, serving as the medium in which fermentation occurs. Its quality can significantly influence the outcome of the ferment, as chlorine and other chemicals present in tap water can inhibit microbial activity. Thus, many fermenters prefer filtered or spring water to ensure the health and vitality of the fermentation culture. In lacto-fermentation of vegetables, water mixed with salt creates a brine that submerges and preserves the food while creating an anaerobic environment conducive to fermentation.

Salt is indispensable in many fermentation processes, particularly in the lacto-fermentation of vegetables like sauerkraut, kimchi, and pickles. Salt draws water out of the vegetables, forming a brine that inhibits the growth of harmful bacteria while promoting the proliferation of lactobacilli. Beyond its preservative qualities, salt enhances flavor and contributes to the crunchy texture of fermented vegetables. The type of salt used is essential; most fermenters prefer non-iodized salt without anti-caking agents, as these can interfere with the fermentation process.

Cultures, or starters, are often added to initiate fermentation. These can be wild cultures naturally present on the ingredients or in the environment, as is the case with sourdough bread and traditional vegetable ferments. Alternatively, they can be specific strains of bacteria or yeast introduced to the ferment, such as the SCOBY (symbiotic culture of bacteria and yeast) used in kombucha or the cultures added to milk to make yogurt and cheese. These cultures are the workhorses of fermentation, each imparting distinct flavors and textures to the finished product.

Spices and herbs are frequently used to flavor fermented foods, adding complexity and depth to the finished products. Each culture has its traditional spice blends that characterize its fermented foods, from the chili peppers and garlic in kimchi to the dill and garlic in pickles. These ingredients not only contribute flavor but can also have antimicrobial properties that support the fermentation process.

Vinegar is sometimes used in fermentation, particularly in quick pickling, where it creates an acidic environment that preserves the food. While not a ferment in itself, vinegar can be produced through the fermentation of ethanol by acetic acid bacteria, resulting in products like apple cider vinegar and balsamic vinegar, which are then used in culinary applications, including some fermentation processes.

In conclusion, the common ingredients used in fermentation – carbohydrates, water, salt, cultures, and flavorings like spices and herbs – play fundamental roles in the success and character of fermented foods and beverages. Each ingredient contributes to the complex interplay of chemistry and microbiology that defines fermentation, influencing everything from the speed of fermentation to the flavor, texture, as well as nutritional value of the final product. As we continue to explore and innovate within fermentation, these basic ingredients serve as the building blocks for an endless variety of fermented goods, which reflects the rich tapestry of human culture and culinary tradition. By fermenting these ingredients, we tap into an age-old practice that nourishes, preserves, and delights, connecting us to generations past and to communities around the globe.

Safety precautions when fermenting

Fermentation is a time-honored culinary practice that has been utilized for centuries to preserve food, enhance flavors, and enrich diets with probiotics. While fermentation is a relatively safe method of food preservation, certain safety precautions must be observed to ensure that the process yields delicious and healthful results. These precautions are essential to prevent contamination, spoilage, and the growth of harmful bacteria. This section explores the critical safety measures one must consider when engaging in fermentation, offering guidance to ensure the safety and success of fermenting endeavors.

First and foremost, cleanliness is paramount in the fermentation process. All equipment, including jars, weights, and utensils, should be thoroughly cleaned and, if possible, sterilized before use. This step is crucial to eliminating harmful microorganisms that could outcompete the beneficial bacteria and yeasts involved in fermentation. A solution of hot water and vinegar or a non-scented, food-grade sanitizer can be used for cleaning. Hands should also be washed thoroughly before handling ingredients or equipment, as they can introduce unwanted bacteria into the ferment.

The quality of ingredients is another critical factor in the safety of fermentation. Fresh, high-quality produce free from mold, bruises, or significant blemishes should be used to minimize the risk of introducing harmful bacteria into the ferment. Using compromised ingredients can lead to spoilage and potentially dangerous outcomes, as the presence of decaying matter can foster the growth of undesirable microorganisms.

When preparing a ferment, creating an environment that favors the development of beneficial bacteria while inhibiting harmful ones is essential. This often involves controlling the salt concentration in brine ferments, such as sauerkraut or pickled vegetables, or the sugar concentration in ferments like kombucha. The correct ratio of salt or sugar to water creates a selective environment that encourages the desired microbial activity. Following tried and tested recipes from reputable sources can help ensure these ratios are balanced for safety and flavor.

Monitoring the fermentation environment is crucial to prevent mold growth and harmful bacteria. Fermented foods should be kept submerged under their brine or liquid to limit exposure to air, which can introduce contaminants. In vegetable ferments, using fermentation weights can help keep produce submerged. For ferments like kombucha, ensuring the SCOBY (symbiotic culture of bacteria and yeast) covers the surface of the tea can prevent mold growth. If mold does appear on the surface of a ferment, it's generally safest to discard the batch, as mold can penetrate deeper into the ferment than is visible, potentially producing toxins.

Temperature control is another significant aspect of safe fermentation. Most ferments thrive at room temperature, typically between 65°F-75°F (18°C-24°C). Temperatures outside this range can slow fermentation or promote harmful bacteria growth. In hot climates or during warmer months, finding a cooler spot in the house or using a temperature-controlled fermentation chamber can help maintain an optimal fermentation environment. pH levels are a critical safety measure in many fermentation processes, especially in preventing botulism, a rare but potentially fatal illness caused by

Clostridium botulinum toxins. The acidic environment produced during fermentation generally inhibits the growth of C. botulinum. However, ensuring the pH of the fermented product is below 4.6 is necessary for safety. Using pH strips or a digital pH meter to monitor acidity can assure that the ferment is within a safe range.

Finally, understanding and recognizing the signs of successful fermentation versus spoilage is key to ensuring the safety of fermented foods. Healthy fermentation signs include bubbles, a tangy smell, and a slightly sour taste. Any off odors, colors, or flavors, such as a rancid or putrid smell, can indicate spoilage and mean the ferment should be discarded. Knowledge and attentiveness are vital in distinguishing between a safe, successful ferment and one that could pose a health risk.

In conclusion, while fermentation is generally safe and rewarding, adhering to safety precautions is crucial for producing high-quality, healthful fermented foods. Cleanliness, quality of ingredients, environmental control, and vigilance in monitoring the fermentation process are all essential steps in mitigating risks and ensuring the success of fermentation projects. By following these guidelines, enthusiasts can confidently explore the vast world of fermentation, enjoying the myriad flavors, textures, and health benefits that fermented foods offer.

CHAPTER V

Fermentation Techniques

Fermenting vegetables

Fermenting vegetables is a practice as ancient as agriculture itself. It is a magical process through which simple vegetables are transformed into flavorful, probiotic-rich superfoods. This section explores the multifaceted world of vegetable fermentation, delving into the science behind it, the benefits it offers, and the diverse traditions it encompasses. It is a journey through time and culture, highlighting how this age-old preservation method has become a cornerstone of healthy diets worldwide.

At its core, fermenting vegetables involves a relatively straightforward process: submerging vegetables in a brine or allowing them to ferment in their own juices, typically with the addition of salt, to create an environment where beneficial bacteria can thrive. These bacteria, primarily from the Lactobacillus family, initiate the fermentation process by converting sugars and starches present in the vegetables into lactic acid. This lactic acid provides fermented vegetables their distinct sour flavor and serves as a natural preservative by preventing the growth of harmful bacteria.

The science of vegetable fermentation is rooted in the principle of anaerobic metabolism. In the absence of oxygen, lactobacilli metabolize the sugars found in vegetables, producing lactic acid as a byproduct. This acidification of the environment not only preserves the vegetables, making them safe for consumption over extended periods, but also enhances their nutritional profile. Fermented vegetables are rich in vitamins, particularly vitamin C and B vitamins, and are a source of essential minerals and dietary fiber. Moreover, fermentation generates probiotics, beneficial bacteria that contribute to a healthy gut microbiome, helping digestion and bolstering the immune system.

The benefits of fermenting vegetables extend beyond nutrition and preservation. Fermentation also unlocks new textures and complex flavors, transforming ordinary vegetables into culinary delights. From the crisp tanginess of sauerkraut to the spicy depth of kimchi, fermented vegetables offer a palette of flavors that can enhance any meal. These fermented products can serve as condiments, side dishes, or flavorful ingredients in their own right, adding zest and complexity to a wide range of culinary creations.

Culturally, fermenting vegetables is a practice steeped in tradition, varying widely across different societies. Each culture has developed its own methods and recipes, often passed down through generations. In Eastern Europe, for example, sauerkraut is a staple, made by fermenting cabbage with salt and sometimes caraway seeds. Korean cuisine boasts kimchi, a fermented mixture of vegetables, most typically napa cabbage and Korean radishes, seasoned with chili pepper, garlic, ginger, and scallions. Meanwhile, in Japan, tsukemono refers to a wide variety of pickled vegetables, each with its unique preparation method and set of flavors. These traditions reflect the culinary heritage of their respective cultures and their ingenuity in using fermentation to enhance diet and health.

Despite the regional differences in methods and flavors, the fundamental principles of fermenting vegetables remain consistent. The process begins with selecting high-quality, fresh vegetables. Cleanliness is paramount;

all equipment and containers used in fermentation must be thoroughly cleaned to prevent contamination. Vegetables are then cut or shredded, mixed with salt, and tightly packed into fermentation vessels, such as glass jars or ceramic crocks. The salt draws out water from the vegetables, creating a brine that submerges them, thus creating an anaerobic environment conducive to fermentation. Depending on the temperature and specific recipe, the vegetables will ferment for several days to several weeks until the desired flavor and acidity are achieved.

Safety is a critical consideration in fermenting vegetables. Proper sanitation, the correct ratio of salt to vegetables, and ensuring that the vegetables remain submerged in brine are all essential measures to prevent spoilage and the growth of harmful bacteria. Observing the fermentation process, looking out for signs of spoilage which include mold or off odors, and tasting the ferment at various stages can help ensure a safe and successful fermentation.

In conclusion, fermenting vegetables is an art that marries the simplicity of basic ingredients with the complex interplay of microbiology and flavor science. It is a testament to human ingenuity, a practice that has not only stood the test of time but has also gained renewed interest in today's health-conscious society. Fermented vegetables enrich our diets with probiotics, vitamins, and flavors that cannot be achieved through any other means of preparation. They connect us to our ancestors and cultures around the globe, reminding us of the shared human endeavor to nourish ourselves physically, spiritually, and culturally. As we explore and innovate within the realm of vegetable fermentation, we tap into the endless possibilities that this ancient technique offers for enhancing health, flavor, and cultural connection.

Fermenting fruits

Fermenting fruits, a practice as ancient as civilization itself, is a testament to humanity's ingenuity in food preservation and flavor enhancement. This transformative process, rooted in the natural activity of microorganisms, not only extends the shelf life of perishable fruits but also enriches them with unique flavors, textures, and health benefits. This section delves into the art and science of fermenting fruits, exploring the biochemical mechanisms at play, the diverse cultural traditions that embrace it, and the myriad benefits it offers to the modern diet.

At the heart of fruit fermentation is the conversion of sugars into alcohol, carbon dioxide, and organic acids by yeast and bacteria. This metabolic activity occurs under anaerobic conditions, where oxygen is limited, creating an environment conducive to the proliferation of specific microorganisms beneficial to the fermentation process. The most familiar products of fruit fermentation are alcoholic beverages such as wine, cider, and perry, which result from the action of yeast on the natural sugars found in grapes, apples, and pears, respectively. However, the spectrum of fermented fruit products extends far beyond these well-known drinks, encompassing various vinegars, condiments, and even pickled fruits.

The biochemical foundation of fruit fermentation is shared across various methods, yet the outcomes can be remarkably diverse. Yeasts, primarily of the Saccharomyces species, are the main agents in alcoholic fermentation, converting fructose and glucose into ethanol and carbon dioxide. This process not only preserves the fruit by inhibiting the growth of spoilage-causing microorganisms but also contributes to the complex flavors and aromas characteristic of fermented fruit beverages. In addition to alcoholic fermentation, some fruit fermentations involve lactic acid bacteria, which transform sugars into lactic acid, enriching the fruit with tangy flavors and improving digestibility.

Fermented fruit products are celebrated in cultures around the globe, each with its unique preparations and traditions. In Georgia, the ancient practice of making wine in qvevris, large earthenware vessels buried underground, showcases the deep cultural significance of fermented grapes. In East Asia, fermented plums and umeboshi are staples, prized for their sour and salty taste profile and purported health benefits. The versatility of fermented fruits is also evident in the culinary use of vinegars derived from fruit fermentation, such as apple cider vinegar, which is used not only as a condiment but also for its health-promoting properties.

The benefits of fermenting fruits extend beyond preservation and flavor enhancement. Fermented fruits are rich in probiotics, beneficial bacteria that are crucial to gut health and overall well-being. These microorganisms can aid digestion, boost the immune system, and even contribute to mental health through the gut-brain axis. Furthermore, the fermentation process can increase the bioavailability of nutrients in fruits, making vitamins and minerals more accessible to the body. The production of organic acids during fermentation also adds a layer of safety, establishing an acidic environment that prevents dangerous microorganisms from growing.

Despite the many advantages, fermenting fruits requires careful attention to ensure safety and quality. The selection of fresh, high-quality fruits free from spoilage is crucial, as the presence of unwanted microorganisms can lead to off-flavors or spoilage. Cleanliness in the fermentation environment and equipment is paramount to prevent contamination. Additionally, controlling the fermentation temperature and duration is vital to achieve the desired balance of sweetness, acidity, and alcohol content. Monitoring the progress of fermentation, including the development of flavors and yeast activity, allows adjustments to be made to ensure a successful ferment.

The practice of fermenting fruits also reflects a commitment to sustainability and the wise use of resources. By transforming surplus or imperfect fruits that might otherwise be wasted into valuable fermented products, this process contributes to reducing food waste. Moreover, homemade fruit fermentations can minimize reliance on commercially produced goods, offering a more sustainable and personalized approach to consumption. In conclusion, fermenting fruits is a rich and multifaceted practice that bridges the gap between ancient traditions and contemporary culinary innovation. It harnesses the power of microorganisms to transform the simple sugars in fruits into an array of delightful and healthful products, from intoxicating beverages to tangy condiments. This process extends the life of perishable fruits and elevates them to new heights of flavor and nutritional value. As we continue to explore and experiment with fruit fermentation, we tap into a deep well of cultural heritage, celebrating the diversity and creativity of human cuisine. Whether for the novice home fermenter or the seasoned culinary professional, fermenting fruits offers endless enrichment, discovery, and enjoyment possibilities.

Fermenting grains and legumes

Fermenting grains and legumes represents a convergence of tradition, nutrition, and culinary innovation, embodying an ancient practice that enriches diets and cultures worldwide. This preservation and flavor enhancement method extends the shelf life of these staple foods and unlocks many health benefits, making grains and legumes more digestible and their nutrients more accessible. This section delves into the fascinating world of fermenting grains and legumes, exploring the processes involved, their historical and cultural significance, and their myriad benefits.

Fermenting grains and legumes involves the metabolic action of microorganisms including bacteria, yeasts, and molds, which convert carbohydrates into alcohol, organic acids, and other compounds. This transformation occurs under anaerobic conditions, where the absence of oxygen facilitates the proliferation of beneficial microbes. The most common products of this fermentation are lactic acid and ethanol, which act as natural preservatives and contribute to the distinct flavors and textures of fermented foods. Notable examples include sourdough bread, made from naturally fermented grain dough, and tempeh, a fermented soybean product which is a staple in Indonesian cuisine.

Historically, the fermentation of grains and legumes has been crucial in human nutrition and survival. These methods allowed ancient civilizations to store surplus harvests for leaner times, ensuring a continuous food supply. In regions where fresh produce was scarce or seasonal, fermented grains and legumes provided essential nutrients and probiotics, contributing to the health and well-being of the population. Over time, these practices have evolved, integrating into various cultural traditions and giving rise to various fermented foods that reflect different communities' unique flavors and culinary heritage.

The fermentation of grains and legumes offers several nutritional benefits. It improves the bioavailability of nutrients, making vitamins, minerals, and amino acids more accessible to the body. For example, the fermentation process can reduce the presence of phytic acid, a compound found in grains and legumes that binds minerals such as iron, zinc, and calcium, preventing their absorption. Additionally, fermentation can increase the content of B vitamins, particularly B12, which is often lacking in vegetarian and vegan diets. The process also generates probiotics, beneficial bacteria that aid gut health and enhance the immune system.

Beyond nutrition, fermenting grains and legumes also improves digestibility. The breakdown of complex carbohydrates and proteins during fermentation produces simpler molecules that are easier for the body to process. This can alleviate digestive issues including bloating and gas associated with consuming legumes and grains. Furthermore, fermentation can neutralize or reduce the levels of anti-nutrients and allergens, making these foods more suitable for individuals with sensitivities.

Culturally, fermented grains and legumes are celebrated in cuisines around the globe. Injera, which is a sourdough flatbread that is made from teff grain, is a cornerstone of

Ethiopian and Eritrean meals. Natto, fermented soybeans with a distinctive sticky texture and strong flavor, is a traditional Japanese food known for its health benefits. These and many other fermented products are dietary staples and carry cultural and historical significance, symbolizing the ingenuity and adaptability of human culinary practices.

Despite the many advantages, fermenting grains and legumes requires careful attention to ensure safety and quality. The choice of fermentation starter, whether naturally occurring microbes or added cultures, can influence the outcome of the fermentation process. Controlling environmental factors which include temperature and humidity is vital to encourage the growth of beneficial microorganisms while inhibiting harmful ones. Moreover, observing proper hygiene and sanitation practices is crucial to prevent contamination.

In conclusion, fermenting grains and legumes is a practice that transcends mere food preservation, representing a harmonious blend of nutrition, tradition, and gastronomy. It showcases the remarkable ability of microorganisms to transform basic ingredients into foods that are more nutritious, digestible, and flavorful. As we continue to explore and embrace the diversity of fermented foods, we nourish our bodies and connect with the rich tapestry of human culture, celebrating the shared heritage of fermentation. Whether for health, flavor, or sustainability, the fermentation of grains and legumes stands as a testament to the enduring relevance of this ancient culinary art in the modern world.

Fermenting dairy products

Fermenting dairy products is an ancient practice that transcends cultures and geography, a testament to humanity's ingenuity in food preservation and health enhancement. This process, rooted in the biology of beneficial microorganisms, transforms milk into various products with extended shelf life, enhanced flavors, and nutritional benefits. From the tangy thickness of yogurt to the sharp richness of cheese, fermented dairy products are revered in global cuisines and nutrition. This section delves into the art and science of fermenting dairy, exploring the processes involved, their historical significance, and their myriad health benefits.

The process of fermenting dairy products begins by introducing specific bacteria, yeasts, or molds to milk. These microorganisms feed on lactose, the sugar present in milk, converting it into lactic acid. This acidification process gives fermented dairy products their characteristic tang and acts as a natural preservative by lowering the pH and inhibiting the growth of harmful bacteria. The most common microbes involved in dairy fermentation are Lactobacillus, Streptococcus, and Bifidobacterium species, each contributing its unique flavor and textural profiles to the final product.

Historically, dairy fermentation has been crucial in human nutrition and cultural development. It allowed for the safe storage of milk, a highly perishable commodity, especially in pre-refrigeration times. Nomadic cultures, in particular, developed various fermented dairy products to preserve the nutritional value of milk obtained from their herds. These traditional practices gave rise to diverse products, including kefir, a fermented milk drink from the Caucasus Mountains, and kumis, a slightly alcoholic beverage made from mare's milk in Central Asia. Each of these products symbolizes the culinary ingenuity of their respective cultures and highlights the role of fermentation in sustaining communities through times of scarcity.

The benefits of fermenting dairy extend well beyond preservation. Fermented dairy products are renowned for their probiotic content, live microorganisms that confer health benefits to the host when consumed in adequate amounts. These probiotics play a vital role in gut health, aiding digestion, and enhancing the immune system. Additionally, the fermentation process breaks down lactose, making these products more digestible for individuals with lactose intolerance. The reduction in lactose content allows those who might otherwise avoid dairy to enjoy the rich flavors and nutritional benefits of fermented dairy products.

Moreover, fermented dairy products are rich in vitamins, minerals, and proteins. The fermentation process can increase the levels of specific B vitamins, including riboflavin and B12, which are essential for energy metabolism and keeping healthy blood and nerve cells. The high-quality proteins found in fermented dairy, such as casein and whey, provide essential amino acids that are important for growth, repair, and maintenance of body tissues. The presence of calcium and phosphorus, key minerals for bone health, further underscores the nutritional value of these products.

Despite their health benefits, fermenting dairy products at home requires meticulous attention to ensure safety and quality. The selection of starter cultures is crucial; commercially available cultures designed for home fermentation can offer more predictable results and reduce the risk of contamination. Maintaining cleanliness in the fermentation environment, including sterilizing equipment and containers, is essential to prevent the introduction of harmful bacteria. Temperature control is another critical factor; most dairy fermentations require warm, consistent temperatures to encourage the growth of beneficial bacteria while preventing the proliferation of unwanted microbes.

Culturally, fermented dairy products hold significant culinary and symbolic value. They are integral to traditional diets, used in cooking, as condiments, or enjoyed independently. In many cultures, these products are associated with festivities, religious ceremonies, and community gatherings, highlighting their importance beyond mere sustenance. The global popularity of fermented dairy, from Greek yogurt to Italian cheeses, reflects a shared appreciation for the depth of flavor and richness these products bring to the table.

In conclusion, fermenting dairy products is a practice that melds the ancient art of preservation with modern understandings of nutrition and health. It demonstrates the transformative power of microorganisms, turning simple milk into an array of delicious, healthful foods. As we continue to explore the possibilities of dairy fermentation, we celebrate the culinary diversity of our global heritage and embrace the health benefits these fermented products offer. Whether enjoyed as a staple of daily nutrition or savored as a delicacy, fermented dairy products represent a confluence of culture, science, and artistry that continues to enrich our diets and lives.

Fermenting beverages

Fermenting beverages is an art that threads through the tapestry of human history, intertwining with the cultural, social, and nutritional fabric of societies worldwide. This ancient practice, which harnesses the transformative power of yeast and bacteria, turns simple ingredients—water, grains, fruits, and honey—into complex drinks that range from mildly effervescent to richly alcoholic. This section explores the multifaceted world of fermented beverages, delving into the processes underpinning their creation, their historical significance, and the global traditions that celebrate them.

At the core of fermenting beverages is the biological process of fermentation, where microorganisms such as yeast and bacteria metabolize sugars, producing alcohol, carbon dioxide, and other compounds as byproducts. This process not only extends the shelf life of the beverage but also enriches it with flavors, aromas, and textures that are impossible to achieve through other means. The type of microorganism, the source of sugars, and the fermentation conditions all play critical roles in identifying the character of the final product, be it beer, wine, kombucha, or kefir.

Historically, the production of fermented beverages dates back thousands of years, with evidence of early beer brewing and wine making found in ancient Mesopotamia and Egypt. These beverages were not only dietary staples, providing essential calories and nutrients, but also held ceremonial and medicinal roles. In many cultures, fermented beverages were believed to have divine properties, bridging the earthly with the spiritual. The act of fermentation, seen as a mysterious transformation of mundane ingredients into something vibrant and alive, was often shrouded in ritual and reverence.

The diversity of fermented beverages across cultures is staggering. In Europe, beer and wine have dominated the scene for centuries, each region developing its unique styles through local ingredients and brewing traditions. Asia offers a plethora of rice-based beverages, such as sake in Japan and makgeolli in Korea, each with its distinct brewing methods and occasions for consumption. In Africa, traditional beers and wines are made from sorghum, millet, and bananas, reflecting different regions' agricultural practices and culinary preferences. The Americas have contributed with beverages like pulque, a milky, slightly foamy alcoholic drink made from the fermented sap of the agave plant, deeply rooted in the indigenous cultures of Mexico.

Fermented beverages offer more than just sensory pleasure; they also carry health benefits, particularly those that are lightly fermented and contain live probiotics. Beverages like kombucha, a fermented tea, and kefir, a fermented milk drink, are touted for their gut-health-promoting properties, including aiding digestion and bolstering the immune system. The probiotics present in these drinks contribute to a healthy microbiome, underlining the connection between diet, fermentation, and wellness.

Despite their benefits, fermented beverages require careful control and understanding of the fermentation process to ensure safety and achieve the desired flavors. Contamination by unwanted microorganisms can spoil the beverage and pose health risks. As such, cleanliness and sanitation are paramount in the fermenting process, from preparing ingredients to sealing the final product. Temperature control is another critical factor; different microorganisms thrive at different temperatures, influencing the rate and character of fermentation.

In recent years, there has been a resurgence of interest in traditional and artisanal fermented beverages, driven by a desire for natural, probiotic-rich drinks and a fascination with the rich flavors and cultural stories they carry. Home brewing and fermenting have become popular hobbies, allowing individuals to explore fermentation's creative possibilities and connect with ancient traditions in their kitchens.

The global landscape of fermented beverages is a testament to human creativity and our enduring relationship with the microscopic world. From the ancient beers of Mesopotamia to the modern craft breweries, from traditional rice wines to experimental kombucha flavors, fermented beverages continue to captivate our senses and nourish our bodies. They remind us of the communal joy of sharing a drink, the celebration of harvest and abundance, and the simple pleasure of tasting fermentation's complexity.

In conclusion, fermenting beverages is a practice that encompasses a rich diversity of techniques, ingredients, and cultural significances. It stands as a pillar of culinary art, reflecting the ingenuity and adaptability of cultures in transforming basic ingredients into complex, flavorful, and often healthful drinks. As we explore and innovate within the realm of fermented beverages, we pay homage to our ancestors' traditions and contribute to the ever-evolving story of human cuisine. Whether for their taste, health benefits, or cultural significance, fermented beverages remain a cherished part of our collective heritage, uniting us across time and geography in the shared experience of creation and enjoyment.

Troubleshooting common fermentation issues

Fermentation, a process as ancient as civilization itself, is a delicate dance between microorganisms and the foods we wish to transform. While often rewarding, this process can present challenges even to the most experienced fermenters. Understanding and troubleshooting common fermentation issues are essential skills for anyone looking to master this art. This section delves into some of the frequent hurdles encountered during fermentation and provides guidance on how to address them, ensuring successful and flavorful ferments.

One common issue in fermentation is the lack of activity, where the expected bubbles or signs of fermentation are absent. This problem often arises due to an environment that is too cold, which can slow down or completely halt the activity of yeast and bacteria. To remedy this, fermenters can move their fermentation vessel to a warmer spot, ideally between 65°F-75°F (18°C-24°C) for most ferments. Another cause of inactivity could be the use of chlorinated tap water, which can inhibit microbial growth. Using filtered or spring water instead can resolve this issue.

Another frequent challenge is mold growth, which can occur when ferments are exposed to air or if the fermentation environment is not clean. Mold typically appears as fuzzy spots on the surface of the ferment and can introduce unwanted flavors as well as potential health risks. To prevent mold, ensure that the ferment is fully submerged under its brine or liquid, using weights if necessary. Covering the ferment with a cloth or airlock lid can minimize exposure to air while allowing gases to escape. If mold does appear, removing the affected portion and ensuring the rest of the ferment is still submerged can sometimes save the batch, particularly in the case of thick ferments like sauerkraut.

Off-flavors or odors are signs that a ferment may not be proceeding as expected. These can result from contamination by unwanted bacteria or yeasts, often due to improper equipment sanitation or the fermentation environment. Ensuring thorough cleanliness and sterilization of all tools and containers before starting the ferment can help prevent these issues. Additionally, tasting the ferment at various stages can help identify any off-flavors early, allowing for corrective measures to be taken.

Another issue that can arise is over-fermentation, where a ferment is left for too long and becomes overly sour or develops an unpleasant texture. This is particularly common in dairy ferments like yogurt or kefir, which can become excessively tart and thin if fermented for too long. To avoid over-fermentation, closely monitor the ferment and taste it periodically, stopping the fermentation process once the desired flavor profile is achieved. Transferring the product to the refrigerator can slow or halt the fermentation for many ferments, preserving the desired taste and texture.

Fermented vegetables that become soft or mushy rather than crisp and crunchy can disappoint many home fermenters. This often results from enzymatic breakdown or over-fermentation. Adding tannin-rich leaves like grape, oak, or horseradish to the ferment can help maintain crunchiness by inhibiting enzymes that soften the vegetables. Additionally, ensuring a proper balance of salt in the brine can prevent over-fermentation and help keep the desired texture.

Yeast blooms or "kahm yeast," a common issue in vegetable and fruit ferments, present as a white or off-colored film on the surface of the ferment. While not harmful, kahm yeast can introduce off-flavors. Maintaining an anaerobic environment by submerging the ferment and minimizing the opening of the fermentation vessel can help prevent its growth. If kahm yeast does appear, it can often be skimmed off the surface without affecting the overall quality of the ferment.

In conclusion, troubleshooting common fermentation issues requires understanding the delicate balance between the ingredients, the microorganisms at work, and the environmental conditions. Addressing problems such as lack of activity, mold growth, off-flavors, over-fermentation, soft textures, and yeast blooms can often be achieved by adjusting temperatures, ensuring cleanliness, monitoring the ferment closely, and maintaining an anaerobic environment. By honing these troubleshooting skills, fermenters can navigate the challenges of fermentation, ensuring successful outcomes that celebrate the flavors, textures, and nutritional benefits of fermented foods. Through patience, observation, and a willingness to learn from each ferment, enthusiasts can deepen their appreciation for this ancient culinary art, continuing to explore its limitless possibilities.

CHAPTER VI

Beyond Basic Pickling and Fermentation

Advanced pickling techniques

Advanced pickling techniques take the fundamental principles of preservation and flavor transformation to new heights, exploring the depths of culinary creativity and science. Beyond the basic vinegar brines and simple lacto-fermentations, these methods delve into complex flavors, textures, and nutritional profiles, offering seasoned picklers a playground of gastronomic possibilities. This section examines the nuanced world of advanced pickling, highlighting the techniques that define this sophisticated craft and how they contribute to the broader culinary landscape.

One advanced technique involves the use of mixed-culture fermentations. Unlike basic fermentations that rely on naturally occurring or single-strain cultures, mixed-culture fermentations use a combination of yeasts, bacteria, and sometimes molds, each contributing unique flavors and textures. This approach allows for a controlled complexity in the final product, where the interplay of different microorganisms can create layers of flavor that are deep and nuanced. For instance, combining lactic acid bacteria with specific yeast strains can yield pickles with a slightly effervescent quality and a rich tapestry of taste that goes beyond simple sourness.

Another sophisticated technique is the utilization of specialized brines, where ingredients such as seaweed, smoked salts, or aromatic infusions are added to the pickling liquid. These brines serve the functional purpose of preservation and impart complex flavors and aromas to the pickled items. For example, a brine infused with oak bark can give pickles a subtle woody note, reminiscent of fine wines aged in oak barrels. Similarly, brines with added sugars or alcohols can develop unique flavor profiles, with the sugars contributing to the fermentation process and the alcohols adding depth and warmth.

Temperature-controlled fermentation represents a further refinement of the pickling craft. By precisely regulating the temperature of the fermentation environment, picklers can influence the fermentation rate and the activity of specific microorganisms. Lower temperatures, for instance, can slow fermentation, allowing flavors to develop more gradually and resulting in a crisper texture. Conversely, warmer temperatures can accelerate fermentation, leading to a more pronounced sourness in a shorter period. This control over temperature enables picklers to achieve a desired flavor, texture, and nutritional content balance, tailoring the fermentation process to their specific goals.

Advanced pickling also explores the realm of pressure fermentation. By fermenting under pressure, specific biochemical reactions are enhanced, and gas solubility in the liquid increases. This technique can intensify flavors, alter textures, and even infuse the pickled items with carbonation, creating a unique sensory experience. Pressure fermentation requires specialized equipment, such as a fermentation chamber capable of withstanding and regulating pressure, making it a more technical and equipment-intensive approach to pickling.

Integrating global pickling traditions and ingredients into advanced techniques offers another layer of complexity and creativity. Drawing inspiration from the diverse pickling practices around the world, picklers can experiment with exotic spices, unusual ingredients, and traditional methods that have been honed over centuries. For example, incorporating Korean gochugaru (red chili powder) into a ferment introduces a vibrant heat and color, while using Japanese umeboshi (salted plums) can add a unique combination of sour, salty, and umami flavors to pickles.

Aged pickling is yet another advanced technique in which pickles are allowed to mature over extended periods, sometimes for months or even years. This aging process can drastically transform the pickles' flavor and texture, developing an unattainable complexity and depth through short-term fermentation. Aged pickles often exhibit a mellowed acidity, enhanced umami notes, and a highly prized richness among aficionados of fermented foods.

In conclusion, advanced pickling techniques offer a fascinating exploration into the art and science of fermentation, pushing the boundaries of flavor, texture, and nutritional value. Through the use of mixed-culture fermentations, specialized brines, temperature and pressure controls, global traditions, and aging processes, picklers can craft products that are both a celebration of tradition and an innovation in culinary arts. These sophisticated methods deepen our appreciation for the complexity of pickled foods and contribute to the ongoing evolution of gastronomy, inviting both makers and consumers to experience the enduring magic of pickling in new and exciting ways. As the practice of advanced pickling continues to grow and evolve, it underscores the limitless potential of fermentation to transform the ordinary into the extraordinary, enriching our tables and palates with each carefully crafted jar.

Experimenting with different fermentation cultures

Experimenting with different fermentation cultures is a journey into the heart of culinary diversity and biological marvel, blending science and gastronomy to unlock previously unimagined flavors, textures, and health benefits. At its essence, fermentation is a transformative process mediated by various microorganisms, including bacteria, yeasts, and molds. Each of these microbial cultures offers unique properties that can significantly adjust the outcome of a fermentation project. This section delves into exploring these diverse fermentation cultures, highlighting their impact on the culinary landscape and the creative potential they hold for enthusiasts and professionals alike.

Central to the fermentation process is the selection of the culture, which acts as the catalyst for biochemical reactions, converting sugars and other carbohydrates into alcohol, acids, and gases. Traditional fermentations often relied on wild or native cultures in the environment or the ingredients themselves. However, with advances in microbiology, a wider array of specific, isolated cultures has become available, enabling more precise control over the fermentation process and its results. This has opened up a vast playground for experimentation, allowing for the creation of novel fermented foods and beverages with distinct characteristics.

Bacterial cultures, mainly lactic acid bacteria (LAB), are among the most widely used in fermenting foods. Species such as Lactobacillus, Leuconostoc, and Pediococcus are renowned for their ability to produce lactic acid, which not only preserves the food but also imparts a tangy flavor and improves digestibility. Each species and strain within these genera can have markedly different effects on a ferment, influencing everything from the speed of fermentation to the specific flavor profiles developed. Experimenting with different LAB cultures can transform simple cabbage into a variety of sauerkrauts or kimchis, each with its unique taste and texture.

Yeast cultures also play a pivotal role in fermentation, especially in producing alcoholic beverages and leavened bread. Saccharomyces cerevisiae, the species commonly used in brewing beer and baking bread, is just the tip of the iceberg. Wild yeasts and non-Saccharomyces yeasts, such as Brettanomyces, offer various flavors and aromas, from fruity to funky. These yeasts can produce complex, layered beverages and bread with qualities that challenge and expand traditional flavor norms. By experimenting with different yeast cultures, brewers and bakers can craft products that stand out for their uniqueness and depth.

Mold cultures introduce yet another dimension to fermentation, playing a crucial role in producing fermented foods such as cheeses, tempeh, and traditional Asian ferments like koji. Molds such as Penicillium roqueforti and Aspergillus oryzae are celebrated for their ability to produce enzymes that break down proteins and fats, contributing to the development of rich flavors and textures. The controlled use of molds in fermentation can result in delicacies with unparalleled complexity, from the pungent depths of blue cheese to the savory umami of soy sauce.

The experimentation with mixed cultures, combining bacteria, yeasts, and molds, represents an advanced frontier in fermentation. This approach can create ferments with a symbiotic complexity, where the metabolic activities of different microorganisms complement and enhance each other. For instance, the simultaneous use of yeasts and LAB in sour beer production can yield a tart and nuanced beverage with layers of flavor that evolve over time.

Understanding the ecological interactions between different cultures is key to successful experimentation. Factors which includes temperature, pH, and nutrient availability can dramatically affect the dominance and activity of certain microorganisms over others. Mastering these variables allows fermenters to steer the fermentation process in the desired direction, achieving specific flavor profiles, textures, and nutritional profiles.

Exploring different fermentation cultures not only enriches the culinary arts but also has the potential to positively impact health and nutrition. Fermented foods are renowned for their probiotic content, which contributes to gut health and overall well-being. By diversifying the cultures used in fermentation, it is possible to enhance the probiotic diversity of foods, offering a broader range of health benefits.

In conclusion, experimenting with different fermentation cultures is an endeavor that bridges tradition and innovation, offering endless possibilities for culinary creativity and discovery. Each culture, with its unique metabolic capabilities, provides a tool for transforming ingredients in ways that deepen our appreciation for fermented foods' flavors, textures, and nutritional values. As we continue to explore the vast microbial world, the potential for new and exciting ferments seems limitless, promising continued evolution in the art and science of fermentation. This exploration contributes to the gastronomic landscape and fosters a deeper understanding of the intricate relationships between culture, food, and health, highlighting the profound impact these microscopic artisans have on our lives.

Incorporating fermented foods into recipes

Incorporating fermented foods into recipes is a culinary practice that marries tradition with innovation, bringing depth, complexity, and nutritional benefits to everyday meals. For centuries, fermented foods, revered for their probiotic qualities and unique flavors, have been part of human diets. As the modern palate becomes increasingly adventurous, integrating these age-old staples into contemporary cuisine offers a bridge between the healthful practices of the past and the diverse culinary landscape of today. This section explores the myriad ways fermented foods can be woven into recipes, enhancing the gustatory and nutritional profiles of dishes across various culinary traditions.

At the heart of this exploration is the understanding that fermented foods possess flavors and textures that are both distinct and versatile. From the tangy crunch of sauerkraut to the creamy depth of kefir, the sourdough's subtle tang to the umami-rich complexity of miso, each fermented ingredient brings its distinct character to the table. These flavors can complement a variety of dishes, acting as a counterpoint to sweetness, enriching savory profiles, or adding a refreshing note to rich, hearty meals.

One of the simplest ways to incorporate fermented foods into recipes is through the use of fermented dairy products like yogurt and kefir. These can be used as bases for smoothies, dressings, and marinades, introducing a creamy texture and a tangy flavor that can elevate the taste of salads, grilled meats, and roasted vegetables. Moreover, the lactic acid present in these products can act as a tenderizer in marinades, breaking down proteins in meat and making them more succulent and flavorful.

With its distinctive taste and chewy texture, Sourdough bread is another fermented food that offers culinary versatility. Beyond its role as a staple at the dining table, sourdough can be used as a base for savory toasts topped with avocado, smoked salmon, or eggs. It can also be transformed into breadcrumbs for coating chicken or fish, adding a subtle tang and enhanced crunch to fried or baked dishes. Furthermore, the leavening power of sourdough starter can be harnessed in pancakes and waffles, contributing to a light, airy texture and a complex flavor profile that sets these breakfast classics apart.

Fermented vegetables, including sauerkraut, kimchi, and pickles, provide a straightforward yet impactful way to introduce fermentation into recipes. These can serve as vibrant accompaniments to meat and fish, adding a burst of acidity that cuts through richness and balances the dish's flavors. They can be chopped or pureed into stews and soups, lending depth and brightness to the broth. Fermented vegetables can also be incorporated into salads, sandwiches, and wraps, offering a crunchy contrast to softer ingredients and imbuing these simple preparations with layers of flavor.

Miso, a fermented soybean paste, is a powerhouse of umami that can transform a wide range of dishes. A small amount of miso can be whisked into soups and sauces, enriching them with a savory depth without overwhelming the other flavors. It can also be used as a glaze for roasted vegetables and meats, where its saltiness caramelizes under heat, creating a rich, complex crust.

Additionally, miso can be incorporated into salad dressings and marinades, where its fermented character adds a nuanced dimension that elevates the dish.

Integrating fermented foods into recipes is not only about flavor; it also offers significant health benefits. The probiotics found in fermented foods contribute to gut health, helping digestion and supporting the immune system. Additionally, fermentation are able to increase the bioavailability of nutrients, making vitamins and minerals more accessible to the body. By incorporating fermented foods into meals, one can enjoy a diverse array of flavors while also nourishing the body with healthful, probiotic-rich ingredients.

In conclusion, incorporating fermented foods into recipes is a practice that speaks to the rich tapestry of human culinary innovation. These ingredients, steeped in tradition and bursting with flavor, offer many possibilities for creative cooking. Whether used as a subtle accent or a central dish component, fermented foods can transform the ordinary into the extraordinary, adding depth, complexity, and nutritional value to everyday meals. As chefs as well as home cooks continue to explore the potential of these age-old staples, the culinary world is enriched, bridging the gap between the healthful practices of the past and the diverse gastronomic landscape of the present. In embracing fermented foods, we celebrate a global heritage of fermentation, weaving its flavors and benefits into the fabric of modern cuisine.

Using pickled and fermented foods in preserving meat

The art of preserving meat through pickling and fermentation is a practice steeped in history, a testament to humanity's ingenuity in extending the shelf life of perishable foods. This method, which predates modern refrigeration, harnesses the power of beneficial bacteria and the acidic environment created by fermentation and pickling to inhibit the growth of spoilage-causing organisms. This section delves into the techniques of using pickled and fermented foods to preserve meat, exploring the science behind these methods, their historical significance, and their culinary possibilities.

At the core of meat preservation through pickling and fermentation is the principle of creating conditions unfavorable for harmful bacteria. The process typically involves submerging the meat in a brine or covering it with a mixture containing pickling or fermenting agents. The high salt concentration in brine draws moisture out of the meat, creating an environment inhospitable to many bacteria. Furthermore, the lactic acid produced during fermentation lowers the pH, further preserving the meat. This dual action not only prolongs the shelf life of the meat but also imbues it with distinctive flavors and textures unique to these preservation methods.

Historically, preserving meat through pickling and fermentation has been crucial for survival, especially in regions with harsh climates where fresh food was scarce during certain times of the year. Civilizations worldwide developed their own methods and traditions for meat preservation, utilizing locally available ingredients to create a variety of preserved meats that could sustain them through the winter months or long journeys. From the corned beef of Ireland to the fermented sausages of Italy and the pickled herring of Scandinavia, each culture has contributed to the rich tapestry of preserved meats that continue to be celebrated today.

The science behind preserving meat with pickled and fermented foods is fascinating, involving a delicate balance of microbiology and chemistry. Introducing beneficial bacteria, such as those found in lacto-fermented vegetables or cultured dairy products, initiates the fermentation process. These bacteria convert sugars present in the meat or added to the brine into lactic acid, ethanol, and carbon dioxide. The acidification of the meat's environment through this process is key to its preservation, as it prevents the development of pathogenic bacteria that could lead to spoilage or foodborne illnesses.

Incorporating pickled and fermented foods into meat preservation enhances safety and elevates the meat's sensory qualities. The acidic components of pickled foods can tenderize meat, breaking down tough fibers and making it more palatable. Fermentation introduces complex flavors resulting from the metabolic activities of the fermenting bacteria, adding depth and richness to the meat that cannot be achieved through other cooking methods. These qualities make pickled and fermented meats highly prized in culinary traditions, offering a distinctive taste experience that is both ancient and profoundly relevant in contemporary cuisine.

One of the key considerations in using pickled and fermented foods for meat preservation is the careful control of environmental conditions. Temperature, humidity, and cleanliness play critical roles in ensuring the fermentation process's success and the preserved meat's safety. Maintaining a cool, stable temperature and a clean working environment minimizes the risk of contamination, while the correct balance of salt, sugar, and acidity in the brine or fermenting mixture ensures optimal conditions for beneficial bacteria to thrive.

In modern culinary practices, the use of pickled and fermented foods in preserving meat has seen a resurgence, driven by a growing interest in traditional food preservation methods and the appeal of artisanal, handcrafted foods. Chefs and home cooks are experimenting with these techniques, establishing an innovative dishes that pay homage to the past while catering to contemporary tastes. Whether it's crafting homemade sausages fermented with kimchi, curing meats in whey from yogurt production, or marinating steaks in kombucha, the possibilities are as vast as they are delicious.

In conclusion, preserving meat with pickled and fermented foods is an art form that bridges the gap between necessity and culinary creativity. This method ensures the safety and longevity of meat and enriches it with unparalleled flavors and textures. As we continue to explore and revive these ancient techniques, we celebrate our culinary heritage and contribute to a more sustainable and flavorful future. Integrating pickled and fermented foods into meat preservation exemplifies the depth of human ingenuity in food science and gastronomy, offering a testament to the enduring value of these practices in nourishing and delighting us through the ages.

Long-term storage and preservation methods

Long-term storage and preservation methods in pickling and fermenting are essential aspects of culinary traditions worldwide, allowing the extension of the shelf life of perishable foods through microbial processes or acidic environments. These methods, deeply rooted in human history, offer practical solutions to food preservation and enrich diets with flavors and nutrients unique to fermented and pickled foods. This section explores the intricate practices of long-term storage and preservation in pickling and fermenting, shedding light on the techniques that have sustained cultures through seasons and across centuries.

At its most fundamental, pickling involves submerging foods in an acidic solution, usually vinegar, or in a saltwater brine, initiating a fermentation process that produces lactic acid. This acidic environment is hostile to spoilage-causing bacteria and molds, effectively preserving the food. For long-term storage, the key is to ensure that the pickled products are kept in conditions that maintain their safety and quality. Traditional methods involve using sterile, airtight containers that are stored in cool, dark places. Sterilizing jars and lids prior to filling is crucial in preventing contamination and ensuring that the seal is airtight, preventing the ingress of air that could spoil the contents.

Fermentation, on the other hand, relies on the action of beneficial bacteria or yeasts to convert sugars as well as starches in foods into alcohol or acids. The byproducts of this metabolic activity, primarily lactic acid in lacto-fermentation, act as natural preservatives. Long-term storage of fermented foods typically involves slowing down or halting the fermentation process to prevent over-fermentation, which can alter the flavor and texture undesirably. This is often achieved by transferring the fermented products to a refrigerator or a cellar, where cooler temperatures slow microbial activity. In some cases, fermented foods can be further processed through canning, which involves heating the food to kill all remaining microorganisms and sealing it in sterile containers.

One advanced method for long-term preservation is pasteurization, which can be applied to both pickled and fermented foods. Pasteurization entails heating the food to a specific temperature for a set period, killing potentially harmful bacteria and extending shelf life. While effective in preserving food, it's important to note that pasteurization also kills beneficial bacteria, including probiotics, and can alter fermented foods' flavor and nutritional content. Therefore, this method is more commonly used for pickled products where the preservation of live cultures is not a priority.

Another critical aspect of long-term storage and preservation is the careful monitoring of pH levels. Maintaining a pH of 4.6 or lower for fermented foods is generally considered safe, as it inhibits the growth of pathogenic bacteria, including botulism-causing Clostridium botulinum. Using pH meters or test strips to monitor acidity levels can help ensure that the preserved foods remain safe for consumption over extended periods.

Vacuum sealing is a modern technique increasingly employed to preserve pickled and fermented foods. By removing air from the storage container, vacuum sealing can greatly lenghtens the shelf life of these foods by minimizing oxidation and the growth of aerobic spoilage organisms. This method is beneficial for fermented foods that have reached their desired flavor profile, as it effectively halts the fermentation process.

The role of salt and sugar in long-term preservation cannot be understated. In pickling, salt is used to create a brine that draws water out of the food, inhibiting the growth of spoilage-causing microorganisms. In fermenting, both salt and sugar can feed the beneficial bacteria, encouraging lactic acid production. For long-term storage, the correct balance of salt and sugar is crucial, as it affects not only the flavor and texture of the preserved food but also its safety.

In conclusion, long-term storage and preservation methods in pickling and fermenting are vital components of food culture and security, enabling the enjoyment of seasonal produce throughout the year and the maintenance of dietary diversity. From the meticulous sterilization of containers to carefully controlling temperature and acidity, each step in these processes is imbued with science and tradition. As contemporary interest in sustainable living and artisanal foods continues to grow, these age-old techniques are being revisited and refined, offering endless possibilities for innovation while staying rooted in the wisdom of the past. Through the lens of long-term preservation, pickling and fermenting reveal themselves not just as culinary practices but as bridges connecting generations, cultures, and communities through the shared experience of nourishing and preserving the earth's bounty.

CHAPTER VII

Health and Nutritional Benefits

Nutritional value of pickled and fermented foods

The nutritional value of pickled and fermented foods is a topic that has garnered increasing attention in recent years, as health-conscious individuals seek to incorporate these traditional foods into their diets. These preservation methods, which have been utilized for centuries across various cultures, not only extend the shelf life of perishable items but also enhance their nutritional profile and introduce beneficial probiotics. This section delves into the myriad health benefits of pickled and fermented foods, exploring how these ancient practices have found a place in modern nutrition.

Fermentation is a metabolic process that happens when microorganisms which include bacteria, yeast, or fungi convert organic compounds—such as sugars and starches—into alcohol or acids. This process is the foundation of many fermented foods and beverages, including yogurt, kefir, sauerkraut, kimchi, and kombucha. The primary benefit of fermentation is the proliferation of probiotics, the beneficial bacteria that are crucial in human health. Probiotics are known to enhance digestive health, improve the absorption of nutrients, as well as strengthen the immune system. These live microorganisms in fermented foods make them a valuable addition to the diet, contributing to a balanced and healthy gut microbiome.

Pickling, while often involving fermentation, can also refer to preserving food in an acidic medium, such as vinegar, without the growth of these beneficial bacteria. Despite this distinction, pickled foods retain and sometimes amplify the nutritional content of the raw ingredients. For instance, pickled vegetables remain a good source of vitamins, including vitamin C and K, as well as minerals such as iron, potassium, and calcium. The acetic acid in vinegar, a common pickling agent, has been shown to have its own health benefits, which include blood sugar regulation and improved heart health.

One of fermented foods' most significant nutritional benefits is their enhanced digestibility. Fermentation breaks down complex carbohydrates, proteins, and fats into more digestible forms. This not only makes the nutrients more bioavailable—meaning the body can absorb them more easily—but also reduces the risk of digestive discomfort accompanying the consumption of certain raw or improperly prepared foods. For example, the lactose in milk is broken down during fermentation to make yogurt and kefir, making these products more tolerable for individuals with lactose intolerance.

Fermented foods also contain unique bioactive compounds, including specific B vitamins (notably B12 in fermented dairy products), omega-3 fatty acids, and antioxidants. These compounds have various health-promoting properties, such as anti-inflammatory and anti-carcinogenic effects. Furthermore, the fermentation process can increase the levels of certain nutrients in foods; for instance, fermented soy products like tempeh and natto are higher in protein and vitamins than their non-fermented counterparts.

In addition to their nutritional benefits, fermented and pickled foods add diversity to the diet through their unique flavors and textures. This can encourage the consumption of a wider variety of foods, contributing to a more balanced and nutrient-rich diet. These foods' tangy, umami, and sometimes spicy flavors can enhance meals and stimulate appetite, making healthy eating more enjoyable and satisfying.

However, it's important to note that not all pickled and fermented foods are created equal. Commercially produced items can sometimes contain high levels of sodium and added sugars, which may counteract some health benefits. Therefore, reading labels and choosing products with minimal added sugars and lower sodium content—or better yet, preparing pickled and fermented foods at home—can ensure that these foods contribute positively to dietary health.

In conclusion, the nutritional value of pickled and fermented foods lies not only in their vitamin and mineral content but also in the presence of probiotics, enhanced digestibility, and bioactive compounds that contribute to overall health and well-being. These foods offer a connection to ancient culinary traditions while providing tangible health benefits in the modern world. By incorporating various pickled and fermented foods into the diet, individuals can enjoy the rich flavors and textures these foods offer while reaping their numerous nutritional and health benefits. As research continues to uncover the complexities of the human microbiome and the role of diet in health, the significance of these time-honored preservation methods becomes ever more apparent, underscoring the wisdom of traditional practices in nurturing health through nutrition.

Probiotic benefits of fermented foods

The consumption of fermented foods and their probiotic benefits is a subject of growing interest in the realms of nutrition and health science. An age-old method of preservation known as fermentation includes the use of bacteria or yeasts and anaerobic environments to convert carbohydrates to alcohol or organic acids. This procedure increases the shelf life of food and adds probiotics, which are live bacteria that, when taken in sufficient proportions, offer a host of health benefits. This section explores the probiotic benefits of fermented foods, delving into their impact on digestive health, immunity, mental well-being, and chronic disease prevention, thereby highlighting their integral role in maintaining overall health.

At the core of the probiotic benefits offered by fermented foods is their ability to enhance gut health. The human gastrointestinal tract houses an intricate community of bacteria, which is known as the gut microbiota, which is crucial in digestion, nutrient absorption, and the synthesis of vitamins. Fermented foods, rich in probiotics, contribute to the diversity and balance of this gut microbiota. By populating the gut with beneficial bacteria, they help outcompete harmful bacteria, reducing the risk of gastrointestinal infections and disorders including irritable bowel syndrome (or IBS) as well as inflammatory bowel disease (or IBD). Moreover, the fermentation process breaks down indigestible fibers, making fermented foods easier to digest and reducing lactose intolerance and bloating symptoms.

Beyond digestive health, the probiotics found in fermented foods significantly impact the immune system. The gut microbiota is intricately linked with the immune system, with a substantial portion of immune cells residing in the gut. Probiotics can enhance immune function by reinforcing the gut barrier, preventing the entry of pathogens, and modulating immune responses. Regular consumption of fermented foods can thus help reduce the frequency and severity of respiratory and gastrointestinal infections, as well as potentially modulate allergic reactions and autoimmune conditions.

The benefits of fermented foods and their probiotics extend to mental health, an area of increasing research interest referred to as the gut-brain axis. This term describes the bidirectional communication between the gut and the brain, mediated by the nervous system, immune system, and hormones. Probiotics from fermented foods might affect this exchange, which may help reduce stress, anxiety, and depressive symptoms. According to some research, some probiotic strains may be able to create neurotransmitters that are involved in mood modulation, like gamma-aminobutyric acid (GABA) and serotonin. Thus, incorporating fermented foods into the diet may support physical and psychological well- being.

Furthermore, consuming fermented foods has been linked to the prevention and management of chronic diseases. The anti-inflammatory properties of certain probiotics can help mitigate the risk factors for diseases such as obesity, type 2 diabetes, and heart disease. Yogurt and kefir, for example, are fermented dairy products that have been linked to enhanced metabolic health, including lower cholesterol and better blood sugar regulation. Additionally, the antioxidant activities of some fermented foods can combat oxidative stress, preventing certain cancers and promoting overall longevity.

Despite the myriad benefits, it is essential to recognize that not all fermented foods contain live probiotics. The processing and storage conditions of commercial products may reduce their probiotic content. To reap the full health benefits, it is advisable to choose products labeled as containing live and active cultures or prepare fermented foods at home under conditions that preserve these beneficial microbes.

In conclusion, the probiotic benefits of fermented foods are manifold, touching upon various aspects of health from digestion as well as immunity to mental well-being and chronic disease prevention. These foods offer a delicious and natural way to support the body's functions, rooted in age-old culinary traditions yet backed by modern science. As research continues to unravel the complex interactions between diet, gut microbiota, and health, the value of fermented foods and their probiotics becomes ever more apparent. Incorporating a variety of these foods into one's diet can contribute to a balanced, healthful lifestyle, exemplifying the adage that good health truly begins in the gut. Through the lens of fermented foods, we are reminded of the power of nutrition to heal, protect, and nourish the body, celebrating the profound connection between what we eat and how we feel.

How pickling and fermentation aid digestion

Pickling and fermentation are time-honored culinary practices that preserve food and enhance its nutritional value, particularly in aiding digestion. These methods involve natural processes that transform the food's chemical makeup, making it more digestible and increasing the availability of nutrients. This section explores the digestive benefits of pickled and fermented foods, delving into the scientific mechanisms behind these benefits, the role of probiotics and enzymes, and the impact on gut health and overall well-being.

At the heart of the digestive benefits offered by pickling and fermentation is the process of lacto-fermentation, where in natural bacteria feed on the sugar and also starch in the food, developing lactic acid. This method not only preserves the food but also produces beneficial enzymes, b-vitamins, Omega-3 fatty acids, and various strains of probiotics. Probiotics, the live bacteria found in fermented foods, are known to enhance the gut flora, or microbiome, which is crucial for healthy digestion. The human gut hosts a complex community of over 100 trillion microbial cells which play a significant role in digesting food, absorbing nutrients, and forming the body's immune system. By consuming fermented foods, one introduces beneficial bacteria into the gut, thereby promoting a healthy digestive ecosystem.

The process of fermentation pre-digests the food, breaking down complex molecules into more easily digestible forms. For instance, dairy fermentation into yogurt or kefir breaks down lactose, a sugar that many people find difficult to digest, into lactic acid. This makes fermented dairy products a viable option for individuals with lactose intolerance, letting them enjoy the benefits of dairy without the discomfort. Similarly, the fermentation of grains and legumes reduces phytic acid, an antinutrient that binds minerals, preventing their absorption. Reducing phytic acid enhances the bioavailability of iron, zinc, and calcium minerals, making fermented grains and legumes more nutritious and digestible.

Fermented foods are also high in enzymes that aid in the breakdown of food substances, facilitating smoother digestion. These enzymes act as digestive catalysts, helping decompose food into smaller, absorbable components. The presence of these natural enzymes in fermented foods can alleviate the burden on the digestive system, which sometimes struggles to produce enough enzymes on its own, especially as one ages or due to certain health conditions. Consuming enzyme-rich fermented foods can thus improve digestion and nutrient absorption.

Beyond aiding digestion, regularly consuming fermented foods has been linked to improved gut health. The probiotics in these foods can help balance the gut microbiota, improving gut barrier function and reducing inflammation. A healthy gut barrier prevents harmful substances from "leaking" into the bloodstream and triggering immune responses, a condition known as "leaky gut syndrome." By reinforcing the gut barrier, fermented foods can help prevent gastrointestinal conditions such as irritable bowel syndrome (IBS), Crohn's disease, and ulcerative colitis.

Moreover, the benefits of a healthy gut extend beyond the digestive system. Emerging research implies a connection between the gut health and mental health, often called the "gut-brain axis." The gut microbiota can generate neurotransmitters such as serotonin and gamma-aminobutyric acid (GABA), which regulate mood and emotions. Consequently, by enhancing gut health through consuming fermented foods, one may also experience an improvement in mental well-being, illustrating the holistic benefits of these dietary practices.

Despite the myriad benefits, it is essential to mindfully integrate fermented and pickled foods into the diet. Some pickled foods, especially those not produced through fermentation but instead preserved in vinegar, may have high levels of sodium, which, in excess, may be detrimental. Additionally, individuals with histamine intolerance may need to exercise caution with fermented foods, as they can be high in histamine, a compound that can trigger allergic reactions in sensitive individuals.

In conclusion, pickling and fermentation offer significant digestive benefits, from enhancing the digestibility of food and improving nutrient absorption to promoting gut health and supporting the immune system. These ancient practices, grounded in the natural transformation of food, not only preserve but also enrich our diet with live cultures, enzymes, and nutrients that support optimal digestion. As we continue to uncover the complexities of gut health and its influence on overall well-being, the value of integrating fermented and pickled foods into our diet becomes increasingly evident. By embracing these traditional food preparation methods, we can enjoy an array of flavors while nurturing our digestive health, bridging the gap between gastronomy and nutrition.

Integrating pickled and fermented foods into a balanced diet

Integrating pickled and fermented foods into a balanced diet is known as a holistic approach to nutrition that combines the wisdom of ancient food preservation techniques with modern dietary science. These foods, revered for their unique flavors and health benefits, are not just culinary relics of the past but are increasingly recognized for their role in promoting gut health, enhancing nutrient absorption, and diversifying the palate. This section explores how pickled and fermented foods can be harmoniously incorporated into a balanced diet, contributing to overall well-being and enriching the culinary experience.

Pickled and fermented foods are produced through processes that naturally preserve and transform fresh ingredients. Fermentation, in particular, relies on the action of beneficial bacteria and yeasts to break down sugars and starches in foods, producing lactic acid, alcohol, and carbon dioxide. This not only extends the shelf life of the food but also enriches it with probiotics, vitamins, and enzymes. Pickling, often involving the immersion of foods in vinegar or saltwater brine, can also introduce healthful compounds, though the presence of live cultures depends on the method used. Both practices result in foods that offer distinctive tastes and textures, from the tangy crunch of sauerkraut to the sour depth of kimchi and the crisp bite of pickles.

The cornerstone of integrating these foods into a balanced diet is recognizing their nutritional benefits, particularly their contribution to gut health. The probiotics found in fermented foods, such as yogurt, kefir, and lacto-fermented vegetables, play a crucial role in maintaining a healthy gut microbiome. A diverse and balanced gut flora aids digestion, supports the immune system, and may influence mood and mental health through the gut-brain axis. By regularly including fermented foods in the diet, one can support these essential bodily functions.

Moreover, fermentation can enhance the bioavailability of nutrients, making them more accessible for the body to absorb. For instance, fermenting soybeans to produce tempeh increases the levels of bioavailable protein and vitamins, while fermenting dairy into yogurt reduces lactose, making it more digestible for individuals with lactose intolerance. Including a number of fermented foods in the diet can thus ensure a broader intake of nutrients, contributing to a more nutritious and balanced eating pattern.

Incorporating pickled and fermented foods into a balanced diet also involves mindful consumption and moderation. While these foods offer health benefits, they can also be high in sodium, especially pickled products. To keep a healthy balance, it's essential to consider the overall sodium intake from all sources and choose lower-sodium versions of pickled and fermented foods when possible. Additionally, individuals with sensitivity to histamine, a compound that can be present in higher levels in some fermented foods, should exercise caution and select foods that do not exacerbate their condition.

From a culinary perspective, integrating pickled and fermented foods into meals offers an opportunity to enhance flavors and introduce variety. These foods can be used as condiments, adding a burst of flavor to salads, sandwiches, as well as grain bowls. They can also be incorporated into recipes as ingredients, lending their unique tastes to soups, stews, and sauces. For instance, adding a spoonful of sauerkraut to a savory stew can introduce a subtle tanginess, while blending kimchi into a sauce can provide a spicy kick. Fermented dairy products which include yogurt and kefir can serve as bases for smoothies or dressings, contributing both flavor and creaminess.

Balancing the diet with pickled and fermented foods also means exploring the wide range of products available and experimenting with homemade versions. Homemade pickles and ferments allow for customization of flavors and control over ingredients, including the level of salt and sugar used. Engaging in the process of making these foods can also foster a deeper connection to food and an appreciation for traditional food preservation techniques.

In conclusion, integrating pickled and fermented foods into a balanced diet is a multifaceted approach to nutrition that embraces both the health benefits and the culinary diversity these foods offer. One can enrich their diet in meaningful ways by including these foods in moderation, being mindful of sodium intake, and exploring the vast array of flavors and textures available. These ancient preservation methods and contemporary nutritional insights provide a pathway to enhancing gut health, boosting nutrient intake, and expanding the culinary repertoire. As we continue to understand the intricate relationships between diet, health, and well-being, the role of pickled and fermented foods in a balanced diet becomes increasingly significant, offering a delicious and healthful bridge between past and present culinary practices.

Addressing common misconceptions about pickling and fermenting

Pickling and fermenting are ancient culinary practices that have sustained civilizations through the millennia, enabling our ancestors to preserve the bounty of harvests and enjoy flavorsome, nutritious foods year-round. Despite their long-standing place in human history, misconceptions about these processes persist, often clouding the understanding of their benefits, safety, and versatility. This section aims to address these common misconceptions, shedding light on the truths behind pickling and fermenting and celebrating the rich culinary traditions they represent.

One prevalent misconception is that pickling and fermenting are essentially the same process, used interchangeably in culinary practice. While both methods preserve food, they do so through distinct mechanisms. Pickling involves preserving foods in an acidic medium, typically vinegar, sometimes with added sugar and spices for flavor. Conversely, fermentation is a metabolic process where natural bacteria feed on sugars in the food,

producing lactic acid, alcohol, or vinegar as byproducts. This crucial difference means that while all fermented foods undergo a form of pickling due to the acidic environment created, not all pickled foods are fermented and contain live cultures beneficial to health.

Another common misconception is that fermented foods are inherently unsafe or pose a higher risk of foodborne illness than other foods. This fear stems from the involvement of bacteria in the fermentation process. However, it is essential to distinguish between harmful bacteria that cause spoilage and the beneficial bacteria involved in fermentation. When proper techniques are followed, the latter dominate, creating an acidic environment that hinders the growth of pathogenic microbes. In fact, fermented foods have an excellent safety record, and instances of foodborne illness from these foods are exceedingly rare when basic hygiene and proper fermentation practices are observed.

There is also a misunderstanding regarding the nutritional value of pickled and fermented foods, with some believing these processes diminish the food's nutritional content. On the contrary, fermenting foods can enhance their nutritional profile. Fermentation can increase the availability of vitamins as well as minerals for absorption, introduce beneficial probiotics that support gut health, and break down compounds that may be indigestible or inhibit nutrient absorption. While pickling with vinegar does not necessarily introduce probiotics, it can still retain or even enhance certain nutrients, depending on the pickling solution and process used.

Another myth is that pickled and fermented foods are too high in sodium or sugar to be considered healthy. While it's true that some pickling and fermenting recipes require salt or sugar, these ingredients are crucial for the preservation process and flavor development. In the case of fermentation, salt inhibits the growth of harmful bacteria, ensuring that beneficial bacteria can thrive. However, many fermented foods can be made with low sodium content, and the sugar in fermented foods is often consumed by bacteria during the fermentation process, which lead to a final product that is not high in sugar.

Mindful preparation and consumption can easily integrate these foods into a balanced diet.

Finally, there's a misconception that making pickled or fermented foods at home is overly complicated or requires specialized equipment. While certain fermentations might benefit from specific tools for optimal results, many pickled and fermented foods can be created with simple kitchen tools and basic ingredients. The revival of interest in traditional food preservation techniques has made information and resources more accessible than ever, empowering home cooks to explore the art of pickling and fermenting safely. With a little understanding and care, anyone can enjoy the process of transforming fresh ingredients into delicious, preserved foods.

In conclusion, addressing these common misconceptions about pickling and fermenting is vital in appreciating these ancient food preservation methods' true value, safety, and nutritional benefits. Far from being outdated or risky practices, pickling and fermenting offer a sustainable, healthful, and flavorful way to enjoy various foods. By understanding the distinct processes involved, recognizing the safety and nutritional advantages, and embracing the simplicity of home fermentation, we can dispel these myths and celebrate the enduring legacy of pickled and fermented foods in global cuisine. As we continue to explore and innovate within these traditions, we enrich our diets and connect with a timeless human endeavor to nourish ourselves and our communities.

CHAPTER VIII

Sustainability and Self-Sufficiency

Importance of sustainable food practices

The importance of sustainable food practices has never been more evident than in today's rapidly changing global environment. As the world grapples with the challenges of climate change, population growth, as well as dwindling natural resources, how we produce, distribute, and consume food comes under intense scrutiny. Sustainable food practices are essential not only for the health of our planet but also for the well-being of current and future generations. This section explores the multifaceted importance of sustainable food practices, encompassing environmental, economic, and social dimensions.

At the heart of sustainable food practices lies the imperative to minimize environmental impact. The conventional food production system significantly contributes to greenhouse gas emissions, deforestation, water scarcity, and biodiversity loss. On the other hand, sustainable agriculture emphasizes the use of practices that maintain and enhance the health of ecosystems. Techniques including crop rotation, organic farming, and reducing chemical inputs like synthetic fertilizers and pesticides help preserve soil health, conserve water, and reduce pollution. Moreover, sustainable practices such as agroforestry and permaculture design work harmoniously with nature, enhancing biodiversity and building resilience to climate change. By prioritizing the environment's health in food production, we can safeguard the natural resources that future generations will depend on.

Economically, sustainable food practices offer a pathway to long-term viability for farmers and communities. Traditional agricultural methods often result in soil degradation, reduced productivity, as well as increased vulnerability to pests and climate variability. In contrast, sustainable practices can improve yield stability and minimize input costs over time, enhancing food security and farmer livelihoods. Furthermore, sustainable food systems support local economies by promoting small-scale farming and reducing dependency on imported goods. This localization of food production and consumption creates jobs, keeps money within communities, and fosters a closer connection between consumers as well as their food sources. In this way, sustainable food practices can be a catalyst for economic development that is inclusive and equitable.

Socially, sustainable food practices address critical

access, nutrition, and health issues. Industrialized food systems often prioritize efficiency and profit over nutrition and equity, leading to diets that are high in calories but low in essential nutrients. Sustainable food systems, by contrast, emphasize diverse crops and animal products that are nutritionally rich and culturally appropriate. By supporting diets based on whole foods and minimizing processed foods, sustainable practices can combat malnutrition, obesity, and diet-related diseases.

Moreover, these practices recognize the importance of food sovereignty and the right of people to healthy and culturally proper food produced through ecologically sound and sustainable methods. Through community-supported agriculture (CSA), urban gardening, and other grassroots initiatives, sustainable food practices empower communities to take control of their food systems, improving access to healthy food and strengthening social bonds.

The ethical dimension of sustainable food practices cannot be overlooked. Issues of animal welfare, fair labor practices, and equitable distribution of resources are central to the conversation around sustainability. Sustainable farming practices often include humane treatment of animals, fair wages and working conditions for farmworkers, and a commitment to social justice. Sustainable food systems promote a more just and compassionate world by addressing these ethical concerns.

The importance of sustainable food practices also extends to cultural preservation and diversity. Food reflects cultural identity and heritage, and sustainable practices support the cultivation of indigenous crops and traditional farming techniques. This not only conserves agricultural biodiversity but also helps maintain the cultural fabric of communities worldwide. In an age of globalization and homogenization, sustainable food practices offer a way to celebrate and preserve the unique food traditions that enrich our global tapestry.

In conclusion, the importance of sustainable food practices is manifold, touching upon environmental, economic, social, and ethical dimensions. As we face the challenges of the 21st century, these practices provide a blueprint for a food system that is resilient, equitable, and harmonious with the natural world. By embracing sustainable food practices, we can ensure the health of our planet and the well-being of all its inhabitants, now and in the future. The journey toward sustainability is collective, requiring the commitment of individuals, communities, and nations. Through informed choices, innovative solutions, and a shared vision of sustainability, we can transform our food systems and forge a path toward a more sustainable and just world.

How pickling and fermentation contribute to self-sufficiency

The practices of pickling and fermentation have long been revered not just for their ability to enhance the flavors of our foods, but also for their contribution to self- sufficiency. In our journey towards more sustainable and independent living, these ancient methods of food preservation stand out as both practical and profound tools. This section explores how pickling and fermentation empower individuals and communities to rely less on commercial food supply chains, reduce waste, and improve nutrition, ultimately fostering greater self- reliance and connection with our food sources.

At the core of their contribution to self-sufficiency, pickling and fermentation extend the shelf life of perishable foods. These processes inhibit the growth of food-spoiling bacteria and fungi by creating an acidic or alcoholic environment, or through the action of preservative compounds produced during fermentation. This allows for the preservation of seasonal bounty, ensuring a stable food supply throughout the entire year, regardless of seasonal changes or unexpected disruptions in food supply chains. For individuals and communities striving for self-sufficiency, this means maintaining a diverse and nutritious diet despite limited access to fresh produce.

Furthermore, pickling and fermentation enhance nutritional value, introducing beneficial probiotics and increasing the bioavailability of nutrients. Fermented foods like yogurt, kefir, sauerkraut, and kimchi are rich in live cultures that support gut health and strengthen the immune system. These foods also often contain higher levels of specific vitamins, such as B vitamins, which are produced by microbial activity during fermentation. By including these foods into their diets, individuals can enjoy improved health and reduced reliance on processed foods and dietary supplements, which are often products of complex, energy-intensive supply chains.

The practice of pickling and fermentation also embodies the principles of zero-waste living, a cornerstone of self-sufficiency. These methods allow for the full utilization of harvests, including parts of fruits and vegetables that might otherwise be discarded. For example, watermelon rinds can be transformed into sweet pickles, and cabbage cores into sauerkraut. This approach maximizes the value extracted from home gardens and local produce and significantly reduces food waste, contributing to a more sustainable as well ad efficient use of resources.

Moreover, pickling and fermentation require minimal specialized equipment and can be made by utilizing simple tools and ingredients. This accessibility empowers individuals to take control of their food preservation processes, rather than depending on commercially processed foods that often come with added preservatives and packaging. The skills needed for successful pickling and fermentation can be easily learned and shared, fostering a sense of community and collective knowledge that strengthens local resilience and self-sufficiency.

In addition to promoting food security and nutrition, pickling and fermentation also encourage a deeper connection with our food systems. Engaging in these practices requires a level of attentiveness and care that brings individuals closer to the rhythms of nature and the cycles of growth and decay. This connection can inspire a greater appreciation for local ecosystems, seasonal eating, and the labor that goes into food production, further reinforcing the values of self-sufficiency and sustainability.

The economic benefits of pickling and fermentation also contribute to self-sufficiency by reducing household food expenses. Preserving seasonal produce when it is abundant and less expensive can lead to significant savings. Additionally, homemade pickles and fermented foods can be superior in taste and quality to their store-bought counterparts, offering a more satisfying and cost-effective alternative. For communities that embrace these practices, the collective savings and increased food security can have a transformative impact, supporting economic resilience and independence.

In conclusion, pickling and fermentation are more than just methods of food preservation; they are pathways to self-sufficiency. By enabling food preservation, enhancing nutritional value, reducing waste, and fostering a deeper connection with our food sources, these practices empower individuals and communities to live more independently. In a world where the sustainability of our food systems is increasingly under threat, pickling and fermentation offer hopeful strategies for resilience, health, and autonomy. As we continue to rediscover and innovate within these ancient traditions, we nurture our bodies, our communities, and the planet.

Using locally sourced ingredients for pickling and fermenting

The resurgence of interest in pickling and fermenting, practices as ancient as civilization itself, reflects a growing awareness of sustainable eating habits and a desire to connect more deeply with our food sources. Central to this movement is the emphasis on using locally sourced ingredients, a choice that not only enhances the flavor and nutritional value of these preserved foods but also supports local economies and reduces environmental impact. This section explores the myriad benefits and considerations of using locally sourced ingredients for pickling and fermenting, highlighting how this practice represents a confluence of gastronomic tradition and environmental stewardship.

The unmatched freshness and quality these ingredients can offer are at the heart of the appeal of using locally sourced ingredients for pickling and fermenting. Local produce, which are harvested at the peak of ripeness, provides the optimal flavor foundation for pickles and fermented foods. The shorter distance between the farm and the table ensures that this produce retains its nutritional value and reduces the carbon footprint associated with transportation. Furthermore, seasonal variations in local produce inspire creativity in pickling and fermenting, encouraging culinary experimentation with various fruits, vegetables, and herbs that might not be available through larger commercial distributors.

Beyond the immediate benefits to taste and nutrition, choosing locally sourced ingredients fosters a closer connection between consumers, farmers, and local food ecosystems. This relationship promotes a deeper understanding of the origins of our food, including the methods of cultivation and the challenges local farmers face. Such awareness can lead to more informed and conscientious food choices, reinforcing the principles of sustainability and food sovereignty. By supporting local farmers and producers, consumers contribute to the vitality of their local economies, ensuring that money spent on food circulates within the community, strengthening its economic resilience.

Using locally sourced ingredients for pickling and fermenting also aligns with the principles of seasonal eating. Seasonal produce reflects the natural growing cycles of the region, often requiring fewer inputs such as water, fertilizers, and pesticides to thrive. Preserving seasonal bounty through pickling and fermenting allows for the enjoyment of these flavors year-round, reducing dependency on out-of-season imports that are typically more resource-intensive. Moreover, seasonal eating connects individuals to the rhythms of nature, fostering an appreciation for the diversity and abundance of each season.

Environmental sustainability is another significant benefit of using locally sourced ingredients for pickling and fermenting. Reducing transportation requirements for local produce significantly lowers greenhouse gas emissions, taking part to efforts to combat climate change. Additionally, supporting small-scale, local agriculture can encourage farming practices that are more harmonious with the environment, such as organic farming, crop rotation, and polyculture. These practices enhance biodiversity, improve soil health, and reduce the ecological footprint of food production.

However, embracing locally sourced ingredients for pickling and fermenting does require a degree of flexibility and adaptability. The availability of certain produce can vary significantly from year to year, influenced by weather patterns, pests, and other factors. This variability encourages a spirit of innovation and adaptability in the kitchen, inviting picklers and fermenters to experiment with different ingredients and techniques based on what is seasonally available. Such an approach not only diversifies the diet but also enriches the cultural tapestry of local food traditions, as recipes are adapted and new ones are created.

In conclusion, using locally sourced ingredients for pickling and fermenting embodies a holistic approach to food that honors our culinary heritage while promoting sustainability, health, and community resilience. This practice offers many benefits, from the enhancement of flavor and nutrition to the support of local economies and the reduction of environmental impact. By fostering a closer connection to the sources of our food, seasonal eating habits, and creative culinary exploration, the use of locally sourced ingredients in pickling and fermenting represents a meaningful step toward a more sustainable and interconnected food system. As we continue to rediscover and innovate within these ancient practices, we nourish our bodies and contribute to the health of our communities and the planet.

Reducing food waste through pickling and fermenting

In a world increasingly aware of the imperative for sustainable living practices, the ancient arts of pickling and fermenting are being recognized for their ability to enhance flavors and preserve food and as vital tools in the fight against food waste. Food waste poses a significant challenge globally, with vast quantities of edible food discarded due to overproduction, improper storage, and the undervaluing of food resources. This section explores how pickling and fermenting can be crucial in reducing food waste, supporting environmental sustainability, and promoting a more conscientious approach to our food resources.

Pickling and fermenting are preservation techniques that extend the shelf life of food items that are perishable by inhibiting the growth of spoilage-causing microorganisms. Through pickling, foods are submerged in an acidic solution, usually vinegar, which creates a hostile environment for bacteria. Conversely, fermentation involves the controlled action of bacteria or yeast to convert sugars into alcohol or acids. Both processes prevent food from spoiling and transform the ingredients into new products with distinct flavors and enhanced nutritional profiles.

One of the most direct ways these practices contribute to reducing food waste is by allowing surplus fruits and vegetables to be preserved. Pickling and fermenting can turn these excesses into delicious, long-lasting provisions, whether it's a bumper crop from a home garden or a bulk purchase from a local farmer's market. This helps in utilizing produce that might otherwise go to waste and building a pantry of preserved foods that can reduce the need for frequent shopping trips, thereby saving time and resources.

Furthermore, pickling and fermenting can use parts of fruits and vegetables that are often discarded. Stems, cores, and peels, which are typically thrown away, can be transformed into pickled delicacies or used in ferments. For example, watermelon rinds can be pickled to create a crunchy, sweet, and sour snack, while the stems of leafy greens can be fermented into tangy, probiotic-rich condiments. This approach encourages a more holistic use of food resources, significantly reducing waste and fostering creativity in the kitchen.

Beyond the level of individual households, pickling and fermenting can also support larger-scale efforts to reduce food waste. Food businesses, from restaurants to grocery stores, can implement these practices to manage surplus inventory and repurpose ingredients that might not meet consumer expectations for freshness or appearance. By integrating pickling and fermenting into their operations, these businesses can minimize waste, lower disposal costs, and create unique products that add value to their offerings.

The environmental benefits of reducing food waste through pickling and fermenting are substantial. Food waste contributes to greenhouse gas emissions, both from the decomposition of organic matter in landfills and from the energy expended in the production, transportation, and processing of wasted food. By preserving surplus produce and utilizing all parts of fruits and vegetables, pickling and fermenting help mitigate these environmental impacts. Moreover, these practices encourage a shift towards more sustainable consumption patterns, emphasizing the importance of valuing and maximizing our food resources.

Adopting pickling and fermenting as strategies to reduce food waste also aligns with broader food sovereignty and security goals. By empowering individuals as well as communities with the skills to preserve food, these practices promote independence from commercial food systems and enhance resilience against disruptions in food supply chains. This is particularly relevant in times of crisis when access to food that are fresh may be limited. The knowledge and application of pickling and fermenting can thus be seen as integral components of a sustainable and self-sufficient food system.

In conclusion, the role of pickling and fermenting in reducing food waste is multifaceted and profound. These time-honored practices offer practical solutions to the global challenge of food waste, turning surplus and underutilized produce into valuable food resources. By embracing pickling and fermenting, we can enjoy the culinary and nutritional benefits they offer, contribute to environmental sustainability, and foster a more mindful and responsible approach to food consumption. As society grapples with the imperatives of waste reduction and sustainable living, the ancient art of pickling and fermenting remind us that the answers to some of our most pressing modern challenges may lie in the wisdom of the past.

Tips for incorporating pickling and fermenting into a sustainable lifestyle

Incorporating pickling and fermenting into a sustainable lifestyle is not just about preserving food—it's about embracing a holistic approach to living that prioritizes mindful consumption, waste reduction, and connection to our food sources. These ancient preservation techniques offer a gateway to a more sustainable way of life, allowing individuals to take control of their food supply, minimize waste, and reduce their environmental footprint. This section explores practical tips for incorporating pickling and fermenting into a sustainable lifestyle, emphasizing the benefits for both individuals and the planet.

First and foremost, embracing pickling and fermenting as part of a sustainable lifestyle requires a shift in mindset towards valuing local, seasonal, and whole foods. By prioritizing fresh, locally sourced ingredients, individuals can reduce the carbon footprint associated with food transportation and support small-scale farmers who practice sustainable agriculture. Shopping at farmers' markets, joining community-supported agriculture (CSA) programs, or growing food in a home garden are excellent ways to access high-quality ingredients while minimizing environmental impact.

Additionally, reducing food waste is a central tenet of sustainable living, and pickling and fermenting offer effective solutions to this challenge. Making a habit of preserving surplus fruits and vegetables through pickling and fermenting not only extends their shelf life but also transforms them into flavorful additions to meals. Using all parts of produce, including stems, peels, and cores, further minimizes waste and fosters creativity in the kitchen. By adopting a "nose-to-tail" approach to fruits and vegetables, individuals can significantly reduce the amount of food that ends up in landfills, thereby mitigating environmental harm.

Furthermore, embracing pickling and fermenting as part of a sustainable lifestyle involves embracing a DIY ethos and reducing reliance on commercially processed foods. Making pickles, sauerkraut, kimchi, yogurt, and other fermented foods at home allows individuals to control the ingredients used, avoid unnecessary additives and preservatives, and minimize packaging waste. Learning basic pickling and fermenting techniques empowers individuals to take charge of their food preservation, fostering a sense of self-sufficiency and reducing dependency on industrial food systems.

Moreover, integrating pickling and fermenting into meal planning and food preparation routines is key to sustaining these practices over time. By setting aside dedicated time for pickling and fermenting, individuals can ensure a steady supply of preserved foods to enjoy throughout the year. Batch cooking and meal prepping with pickled and fermented ingredients can streamline meal preparation, saving time and reducing the need for convenience foods that often come with excessive packaging and waste. Additionally, incorporating pickles, ferments, and their brines into recipes can add depth of flavor and nutritional value to dishes, further enhancing their sustainability.

Another tip for incorporating pickling and fermenting into a sustainable lifestyle is to share knowledge and resources with others in the community. Hosting workshops, exchanging recipes, and participating in food swaps are excellent ways to build a network of like- minded individuals who are passionate regarding sustainable living and food preservation. By fostering a sense of community around pickling and fermenting, individuals can support each other in their journey towards sustainability, share resources and surplus produce, and collectively reduce food waste.

Finally, embracing pickling and fermenting as part of a sustainable lifestyle requires a commitment to continuous learning and experimentation. A wealth of information is available through books, online resources, and workshops on pickling and fermenting techniques, flavor combinations, and troubleshooting tips. By staying curious and open-minded, individuals can expand their culinary repertoire, discover new flavors and textures, and deepen their connection to the food they eat. Embracing pickling and fermenting as lifelong practices allows individuals to cultivate resilience, creativity, and sustainability in their daily lives.

In conclusion, incorporating pickling and fermenting into a sustainable lifestyle is about more than just preserving food—it's about embracing a mindful and intentional approach to living that prioritizes environmental stewardship, waste reduction, and community connection. By valuing local, seasonal ingredients, reducing food waste, DIY food preservation, integrating pickles and ferments into meal planning, sharing knowledge with others, and embracing continuous learning and experimentation, individuals can cultivate a more sustainable relationship with food and contribute to a healthier, more resilient planet. As we continue to navigate the challenges of our modern world, the ancient arts of pickling and fermenting offer timeless wisdom and practical solutions for sustainable living.

CONCLUSION

In closing, "Timeless Pickling and Fermenting: Culinary Skills for the Survivalist" is a tribute to the enduring legacy of pickling and fermenting and a practical guide for modern-day enthusiasts seeking to embrace these timeless culinary arts. Throughout the pages of this book, we have explored the rich history, fundamental principles, and practical techniques that underpin pickling and fermenting, from their ancient origins to their contemporary applications.

By delving into the intricacies of pickling and fermenting, we have uncovered the methods for preserving food and the profound impact these practices can have on our health, sustainability, and self-sufficiency. From the tangy crunch of pickled cucumbers to the funky complexity of fermented kimchi, we have celebrated the diverse array of flavors and textures that can be achieved through these age-old techniques.

Moreover, "Timeless Pickling and Fermenting" has emphasized the importance of embracing sustainable food practices and reducing food waste through pickling and fermenting. By harnessing the power of these ancient preservation methods, we can extend the shelf life of perishable ingredients, utilize surplus produce, and minimize our environmental footprint. In doing so, we nourish our bodies and nurture a more profound connection to the natural world and the rhythms of the seasons.

As we conclude our exploration of pickling and fermenting, I encourage you, dear reader, to embark on your own culinary journey, armed with the knowledge and skills imparted in these pages. Whether you're a seasoned homesteader, a curious novice, or simply someone seeking to embrace a more sustainable lifestyle, the wisdom of pickling and fermenting offers a pathway to greater self-reliance, creativity, and nourishment.

In the spirit of our ancestors who preserved food for survival, let us carry forward the tradition of pickling and fermenting, not merely as a culinary practice but as a testament to our resilience, resourcefulness, and reverence for the timeless wisdom of the ages. May your jars be filled with the vibrant colors and flavors of pickled and fermented delights, and may your journey be enriched by the transformative magic of these ancient culinary arts.

Thank you for buying and reading/ listening to our book. If you found this book useful/ helpful please take a few minutes and leave a review on the platform where you purchased our book. Your feedback matters greatly to us.